VideoHound's

# IDIOT'S DELIGHT

## The 100 Dumbest Movies of All Time

VideoHound's

# IDIOT'S
# DELIGHT

## The 100 Dumbest
## Movies of All Time

DETROIT • WASHINGTON, D.C. • NEW YORK • TORONTO

# VideoHound's Idiot's Delight

ISBN 0-7876-0617-0

**Editors**
Martin Connors
Hilary Weber

**Contributors**
Michelle Banks
Jim Craddock
Beth A. Fhaner
Terri Schell
Devra M. Sladics

**Still More Contributors**
Shawn Brennan
Kelly M. Cross
Julia Furtaw
Christopher Scanlon

**Graphic Design**
Mary Krzewinski

**Photographs**
The Kobal Collection

**Photo Acquisition**
Christine Tomassini

**Photo Editing**
Barbara Yarrow
Pam Hayes

**Production**
Mary Beth Trimper
Dorothy Maki
Evi Seoud
Shanna Heilveil

**Typesetter**
Marco Di Vita
The Graphix Group

*A Cunning Canine™ Production*

# Contents

**Carl:** Looper. You know, a caddy, a looper, a jock. So I tell them I'm a pro jock and who do you think they give me? The Dalai Lama. The twelfth son of the Lama. The robes, the grace. Striking. So I'm on the first tee with him, I give him the driver. He hauls off and whacks one. Big hitter. Long. Into a 10,000 foot crevice. Right at the base of this glacier. You know what the Lama sez?

**Caddy:** No.

**Carl:** Goonga, galanka, gunka gunka, lagunka. So we finish 18, and he's gonna stiff me. And so I said, "Hey Lama, how 'bout a little something, you know, for the effort," you know. And he says "Oh ah, there won't be any money. But when you die, on your deathbed, you will receive total consciousness." So I got that going for me. Which is nice.

CARL, THE ASSISTANT GREENSKEEPER RECOUNTS HIS BRUSH WITH GREATNESS IN *CADDYSHACK*

## Bonus Section!!
### Classic Idiot's Delight

# Introduction

As a public service to cinemaphiles the world over, VideoHound is happy to present *Idiot's Delight: The 100 Dumbest Movies of All Time.* An ambitious undertaking, but one we feel well-qualified to pursue, *Idiot's* is inspired by the rash of recent movie offerings pandering to the brainless (think *Dumb and Dumber). Idiot's* attempts to rank basically silly movies that make us laugh. Out loud. And often. Movies with goofy, eminently quotable dialogue. Movies that spoof, with often hilarious results, more serious movies. Movies that descend to the baser level of guffaws. Movies that are resplendent in their meaningless. In short, movies that take themselves not at all seriously while taking serious aim at the funny bone.

These video gems are returned to over and over again by their fans who, of course, occupy all ages. Many of the movies listed are now regarded as classics: *Airplane!, Young Frankenstein, Sleeper,* and *Monty Python and the Holy Grail,* for instance, are considered comedy standards. Others ranked in the top 100 have not, until now, received their rightful due as very funny movies. Digging deep into the comedy well, VideoHound has unearthed some treasures worth checking out and collecting.

Critics, of course, are generally confounded by such movies, given that many of them (the movies, not the critics) are fairly crude in their approach. The home viewer and the critic have significantly different criteria. Comedy is perhaps the most subjective of the film experiences; what strikes one person as a scream might not even elicit a chuckle from another. Within *Idiot's,* VideoHound surveyed the rich history of cinema, looking for comedies with a modern sense of stupidity that set off compulsive chuckle alerts. Plot, cinematography, and acting we considered extras. The best of the lot are written with a certain flair and cleverness, and are valued for their set pieces and wry asides. Some of the films have had considerable influence on other films, and when that seemed apparent (we didn't dig too deep), we noted it.

To ensure a consistent approach within *Idiot's Delight*, we aspired to consensus by committee. Each movie nominated for the book was viewed by several of the VideoHound staff and then discussed at length. More than 200 movies were originally nominated, and the list was constantly pared down. Other movies came to light as we obsessively watched and laughed. Each of the movies on the list had to have a certain postmodern silliness that transcended the genre; we were looking for movies anarchic and surreal in their use of humor, movies filled with nonsequiturs and preposterous settings, movies with really no point. We didn't want anything smelling of sophistication, or movies with an agenda beyond the obvious.

We discovered that modern comedy included such classics as the Marx Brothers' *Duck Soup* and Jerry Lewis's *The Nutty Professor.* For the films of Chaplin, W.C. Fields, Buster Keaton, and other comedy icons, films that have some richly stupid moments but now seem of a different era, we included a short classic section after the all-time 100.

We also looked for movies that will endure, with high potential for repeat viewings and a certain timelessness. Because with really silly movies, part of the pleasure is returning to them over and over again in a sort of neurotic search for laughs. Movies on the upper level of the 100 are certified as returnables, inspiring a sentimental journey into your own private film history. *Airplane!*, for instance, seems as fresh and funny today as it did more than 15 years ago when first released. Movies on the bottom end of the all-time 100? Well, you be the judge.

Each review includes title, year of release, run time, MPAA rating, cast, director (D), producer (P), cinematographer (C), screenwriter (S), and musical director or composer (M). Nearly 100 classy photos accompany the text, which is not nearly so classy. Sprinkled throughout the text are quotes and trivia concerning the movies. Five indexes authoritatively classify the contents. The appropriately named Title Index arranges the titles alphabetically, at no extra charge. The indexes to cast, director, and writer index the movies by cast, director, and writer, permitting the unsuspecting reader to discover the cross-pollinating talents working in subversive comedy. The category index, a VideoHound staple, consists of 70 or so topics, ranging from **Dense Detectives** to **Homage to Polyester** to **Theme from *Jaws*** (listing flicks spoofing the memorable shark-attack theme).

We hope you find *Idiot's Delight* as entertaining to read as it was for us to put together, and that it leads to fruitful viewing. We look forward to your communiques on the list.

# Airplane!

**(1980) 88m PG**
Robert Hays, Julie Hagerty, Lloyd Bridges, Peter Graves, Robert Stack,
Leslie Nielsen, Stephen Stucker, Ethel Merman, Kareem Abdul–Jabbar
**D:** Jerry Zucker, Jim Abrahams, David Zucker
**P:** Jon Davison and Howard W. Koch Jr.
**C:** Joseph F. Biroc
**S:** Jim Abrahams, David Zucker, Jerry Zucker
**M:** Elmer Bernstein

Let us count the ways *Airplane!* deserves the crown as "Dumbest
Movie of All Time" as voted by the readers of *Good Housekeeping*
magazine. We'll start from the beginning. The opening rip–off of
*Jaws!,* the "red zone/white zone" series of LAX public announce-
ments ("the red zone is for immediate loading and unloading of
passengers only; there is no stopping in the white zone"), and
the increasingly physical encounters with religious fundraisers
in the airport are five good reasons. Jimmy Walker raising the
hood and checking the oil on the jet engine is seven. Then
there's perverted pilot Graves ("Joey, have you ever been in a
Turkish prison?") and Abdul-Jabbar as co–pilot Murdoch, who
emphatically denies that he is the LA Laker star. Every so often
Stucker flies across the screen in camp distress. Add the appropriately wooden portrayals of leads Hays and Hagerty (talk about
your expert casting), shell–shocked war veteran Ethel Merman
belting out a song in a hospital gown, the Beav's mom talking
jive, and an acrobatic spoof of *Saturday Night Fever* in all its
disco glory, and you have comic nirvana. Not only did this lampoon of disaster pics (particularly *Airport* and its subsequent 50+
sequels) and wartime melodramas set a new standard for movies
making fun of other movies, but it seems, like a fine but stupid
wine, to have gotten better with age. With a nod to comedic
insurrectionists Ernie Kovacs, Mel Brooks, The Marx Brothers,
and S.J. Perelman (among others), *Airplane!* gleefully rips into
every Hollywood cliche worth ripping. Hays is Striker, the
straight–arrow ex–fighter pilot who's lost his nerve but is forced
to fly a passenger plane after the crew and passengers are hit

with food poisoning. Flight attendant Hagerty is his ex–girl-friend whom he desperately wants to win back. From the control tower, highly stressed Bridges ("Looks like I picked a bad week to give up sniffing glue") and the near–psychotic Kramer (Stack) try to talk him down. The pace is frantic as sight gags compete with dialogue quips for the viewer's attention. Extremely clever effort by the ZAZ team ignited Hollywood spoof mania. Nielsen's deadpan delivery as the doctor onboard helped launch a new career for him as a comedic actor. Don't hit the rewind button until the final credits are done; it ain't over till it's over. Followed less successfully by *Airplane 2: The Sequel*, a non–ZAZ effort.

> **Striker to the control tower:** Listen to me, Kramer! Doctor Rumack says the sick people are in critical condition and every minute counts. We've got to land now!
>
> **Kramer:** Don't be a fool, Striker. You know what a landing like this means—you more than anybody. I'm ordering you to stay up there.
>
> **Striker:** No dice, Chicago. I'm giving the orders and we're coming in. I guess the foot's on the other hand, now, isn't it Kramer?

*Ground crew anxiously await airplane arrival.*

**Captain Oveur:** Surely you can't be serious.

**Dr. Rumack:** Of course I am! And stop calling me Shirley!

# National Lampoon's Animal House

**(1978) 109m R**
John Belushi, Tim Matheson, Peter Riegert, Donald Sutherland,
Karen Allen, John Vernon, Tom Hulce, Kevin Bacon, Mark Metcalf,
Stephen Furst, Verna Bloom, Bruce McGill, James Widdoes,
James Daughton, Mary Louise Weller, Martha Smith
**D:** John Landis
**P:** Matty Simmons, Ivan Reitman
**C:** Charles Correll
**S:** Harold Ramis, Douglas Kenney, Chris Miller
**M:** Elmer Bernstein

The movie that made stars of Otis Day and the Knights and brought together the money–minting team of John Landis, Harold Ramis, and Ivan Reitman showed that stupid comedy could be sophisticated box office at $100 million plus. Beer, babes, and the barest level of attention to their classwork keep the Delta House slobs rolling at Faber College. The boys skewer every college tradition you can think of ("It's not gonna be an orgy. It's a toga party!") as they battle Dean Wormer (Vernon), the ROTC, and the insufferably snotty Omegas, led by weasely Doug Niedermeyer (Metcalf). Stupidity and depravity are celebrated in swami–like anticipation of anti–PC backlashes, complete with food fights and the homecoming parade from hell. Aspiring studs may want to take notes as Otter (Matheson) shows how to use a tragic kiln accident to pick up women. Stellar ensemble is led by the late, great Belushi as the primitive but inspiring Bluto Blutarsky. Just about every other member of the young cast went on to more sober, somber pursuits, including Riegert, Allen, Hulce, and Bacon, while "Flounder" Furst surfaced again as a confused doctor on TV's *St. Elsewhere.* Written by Ramis, Douglas Kenney, and Chris Miller, it's allegedly inspired by the college exploits of the *National Lampoon* magazine staff. One hopes their alma mater's motto was more inspiring than "Knowledge Is Good." A high energy, anarchic spoof of sixties campus life that's never been topped, *Animal House* still stands as the peak experience in the National Lampoon series.

*Buccaneer Bluto terrorizing fellow Faber frat–boy foes.*

**Bluto:** What the f**k happened to the Delta I used to know?
Where's the spirit? Where's the guts? Huhhh? This could be
the greatest night of our lives. But you're gonna let it be the
worst. Ouuuuuh. We're afraid to go with you, Bluto. We
might get in trouble. Well just kiss my ass from now on!
Not me! I'm not gonna take this! Wormer, he's a dead man!
Marmalard, dead! Neidermeyer...

**Otter:** ....Dead. Bluto's right. Psychotic, but absolutely right. We
gotta take these bastards. Now, we could fight 'em with
conventional weapons, but that could take years, cost
millions of lives. No, in this case, I think we have to go all
out. I think this situation absolutely requires a really futile
and stupid gesture be done on somebody's part.

**Bluto:** And we're just the guys to do it!

# Caddyshack

**(1980) 99m R**
Chevy Chase, Bill Murray, Ted Knight, Rodney Dangerfield, Michael O'Keefe,
Brian Doyle–Murray, Sarah Holcomb, Cindy Morgon, Scott Colomby,
Dan Resin, Henry Wiloxon, Lois Kibbee, John F. Barmon, Jr.
**D:** Harold Ramis
**P:** Douglas Kenney, Jon Peters
**C:** Stevan Larner
**S:** Brian Doyle–Murray, Douglas Kenney, Harold Ramis
**M:** Johnny Mandel, Kenny Loggins

Never had the misfortune of finding yourself wandering about in
the manicured outdoors repetitiously swinging a golf club at a
small dimpled yellow white pink blue ball in the hopes that it
will go into a tiny hole miles away across a river, but you have
the urge? See this masterpiece of fairway foolishness instead; it'll
be a lot more fun and less expensive. Brilliantly written by
two–thirds of the *Animal House* gang (Kenney and Ramis) plus
Brian Doyle–Murray, stupid sports satire delivers inspired lunacy, doing for golf what Dan Quayle did to the vice presidency.
Amid the upper–crust confines of Bushwood Country Club, the
ever–popular, age–old snobs vs. slobs battle royale rages. Affable
caddy O'Keefe copes with girlfriend problems, cheapskate
golfers, family pressures, rival caddies, and the officious Judge
Smalis (Knight) in his quest to get a scholarship. Crazed assistant groundskeeper Carl Spackler (Murray) is every varmint's
nightmare as he dreams of someday winning the Masters ("Cin-
derella Boy, here at Augusta") while tangling with some stub-
born gophers. Nouveau riche developer Al Czervik (Dangerfield)
who hates the stuffy bluebloods almost as much as they hate
him, provides the best non-Carl moments. Chase is at his laconic
best as Zen ("Be the ball, Danny") golfer/playboy Ty, his last truly
funny role until *Fletch* (which was pretty much his last funny
role ever, unless you count some of the *National Lampoon Vaca-
tions,* which some won't but we do). But back to *Caddyshack*:
every set piece works and the hilarious dialogue is quoted like
religious text by the devoted cult who have given up their lives to

*Bushwood's finest compare handicaps.*

do nothing but watch this on video. It could happen to you. Followed by a sequel, *Caddyshack 2*, that makes golf seem interesting by comparison. Dangerfield, Murray, and Knight are replaced by Jackie Mason, Dan Aykroyd, and Robert Stack, respectively, and the comedy is replaced by miniature golf. Well, not really, but who's watching?

**Don't be obsessed with your desires, Danny. The Zen philosopher Basha once wrote, "A flute with no holes, is not a flute. And a donut with no hole, is a danish." He was a funny guy.**

*Ty Webb dispenses life wisdom, such as it is.*

# This Is Spinal Tap

**(1984) 82m R**
Michael McKean, Christopher Guest, Harry Shearer, Tony Hendra, Bruno
Kirby, Rob Reiner, June Chadwick, Howard Hesseman, Dana Carvey, Ed
Begley Jr., Patrick Macnee, Anjelica Huston
**D:** Rob Reiner
**P:** Karen Murphy
**C:** Peter Smokler
**S:** Christopher Guest, Michael McKean, Rob Reiner, Harry Shearer
**M:** Christopher Guest, Michael McKean, Rob Reiner, Harry Shearer

The question is, "How much more funny could this movie be?"
and the answer is "None. None more funny." Hysterical mock-
rockumentary of aging British heavy metal band Spinal Tap
expertly satirizes rock 'n roll pretentions. Documentary filmmak-
er Marty DiBergi (Reiner) follows the band as they limp their way
through a pathetic U.S. tour to promote their new album, "Smell
the Glove," and make a desperate attempt at a comeback. Dates
include a stop at an amusement park where they receive second
billing to a puppet show, a humiliating performance at a military
ball, and a concert in Cleveland where they get lost under the
stage. Interviews with band members reveal their checkered, 17-
year musical career, including the untimely demise of their
drummers (one choked on someone else's vomit and another
spontaneously combusted on stage). None of the scenes were
rehearsed (except the musical numbers) and a great deal was
improvised. The hallmarks of rock are captured with brilliant
accuracy, including the ego trips, childlike delusions, pomposity,
and sexism. This satire is so on target with its portrayal of the real
life absurdity and debauchery of rock bands that it's easy to forget
that *Spinal Tap* is a spoof. At least we think it is.

*Nigel and David go to eleven.*

**T**he Boston gig's been cancelled,
but I wouldn't worry. It's not a big
college town.

*Tap manager Ian Faith*

# The Jerk

**(1979) 94m R**
Steve Martin, Bernadette Peters, Catlin Adams, Bill Macy, Jackie Mason,
Carl Reiner, M. Emmet Walsh, Mabel King, Richard Ward, Dick Anthony
Williams, Dick O'Neil, Maurice Evans, Helena Carroll
**D:** Carl Reiner
**P:** Peter MacGregor–Scott, William E. McEuen, David V. Picker
**C:** Victor J. Kemper
**S:** Michael Elias, Carl Gottlieb, Steve Martin
**M:** Jack Elliott

*The Jerk* stumbles into the top ten based on Martin's sensitive
but stupid portrayal of Navin Johnson and his rags-to-riches-to
rags story. A sharecropper's adopted son who thinks he's black,
Navin yearns to make the leap to simpleton. He sets out on his
own after learning the sad truth of his whitebread origins at the
tender age of at least 30. All that time on the farm didn't particularly leave him an ambassador of world affairs. He sets out for St.
Louis with his dog, Shithead, and somehow manages to find a
job at a gas station and a home of his own in the men's room.
Between wooing his girlfriend (Peters) with the classic "Thermos
Song," surviving a series of screwball attacks by a deranged
killer, and becoming "somebody" upon seeing his name in the
new phone book, he invents the Opti–grab handle for eyeglasses
and becomes a rich, powerful, uh . . . jerk. *The Jerk* is kind of like
*Forrest Gump*, but set in a world more like our own. With his
film debut, Martin began a long and fruitful collaboration with
Reiner, a pairing that proved to be a great combination of 1950's
variety show sensibilities and over-the-top physical comedy.

> **Okay. It was never easy for me. I was born a poor black
> child. I remember the days, sitting on the porch with my
> family, singing and dancing, down in Mississippi.**
>
> *So begins Navin Johnson as he recounts his tale.*

*Navin blows his fortune on hats.*

# Bill & Ted's Excellent Adventure

**(1989) 105m PG**
Keanu Reeves, Alex Winter, George Carlin, Bernie Casey,
Dan Shor, Robert Barron, Amy Stock-Poyton, Ted Steedman,
Rod Loomis, Al Leong, Tony Camilieri
**D:** Stephen Herek
**P:** Scott Kroopf, Michael S. Murphey, Joel Soisson
**C:** Tim Suhrstedt
**S:** Chris Matheson, Ed Solomon
**M:** David Newman

Two most excellent but clueless dudes time surf via a phone booth in order to pass a high school history test. It's undeniably both a stupid and funny movie in an '80s, vapid, Southern California kind of way. Reeves and Winter are boneheaded beach boys who must pass their history final to secure the future of the world. Adventure kicks in as they proceed to capture some of "history's great personages" and manage to mangle most of their names in the process ("Beeth-oven," "So-crates," Sigmund "Frood-dude"). It was the eminently quotable dialogue, in fact, that put "totally," "awesome" and "dude" on the lips of teens nationwide, a totally awesome contribution to the national culture. Highlights include Reeves' brother dissing Napoleon after a trying day babysitting the vertically challenged dictator ("He was a dick"). A big-budget sequel, *Bill & Ted's Bogus Journey*, has better special effects but the laughs are more familiar. Slain by look–alike robot duplicates from the future, the airheaded heroes pass through Heaven and Hell before tricking the Grim Reaper into bringing them back for a second duel with their heinous terminators. Watch for the hilarious closing-credit montage. The Keanu dude, of course, went on to greater and lesser things ranging from Shakespeare to *Speed*, but it takes a sharp eye to catch a film appearance by Winter. In 1993 he starred in a little-seen black comedy called *Freaked*, as a TV star who becomes a sideshow mutant after getting slimed with toxic fertilizer. Buddy Keanu joins him for a cameo as the Dog Boy.

*Keanu Reeves and Alex Winter forget the number for 911.*

# Dumb & Dumber

**(1994) 110m PG**
Jim Carrey, Jeff Daniels, Lauren Holly, Teri Garr, Karen Duffy, Mike Starr,
Charles Rocket, Victoria Rowell, Cam Neely, Felton Perry
**D:** Peter Farrelly
**P:** Brad Krevoy, Steven Stabler and Charles B. Wessler
**C:** Mark Irwin
**S:** Bobby Farrelly, Peter Farrelly, Bennett Yellin
**M:** Todd Rundgren

In essence the inspiration for this book, a film so gloriously stupid that journalists across the country felt compelled to address the issue: "Is America getting dumber?" Well, we can't answer for the rest of America, but certainly we feel more intellectually challenged after watching the movie unwind in all its slow-witted majesty. Although time and marketing will ultimately determine *Dumb and Dumber*'s standing within the pantheon of cinema greats, our deadline forces us to deal with it now. Delving unabashedly (and successfully) where few high-budget movies have gone before, *D & D* takes such pleasure in unselfconscious bathroom jokes, bodily function gags, and slapstick humor that you can't help but laugh. Gross, for lack of a better word, is good. Sporting a Moe Howard-style haircut and a chipped front tooth, moronic limo driver Lloyd Christmas (Carrey) dreams of one day operating a worm farm he'd call "I Got Worms." With equally dense dog groomer Harry Dunne (Daniels), he leaves Rhode Island and heads for the slopes of Aspen in Dunne's van, customized to look like a sheep dog. Their mission: to return a briefcase to a beautiful socialite (Holly). Unbeknownst to the boys, the briefcase is filled with cash and was left as ransom for the woman's kidnapped husband. The kidnappers are now after Lloyd in their race across the country. The plot is the least amusing aspect, however. The main attraction is the silly sophomoric humor from the animated Carrey and mutt-like Daniels as they mug their way to film history, dancing to the beat of a highly entertaining soundtrack.

*New Line Cinema's cash cows.*

**Austria, huh? Well, then. G'day mate.
Let's put another shrimp on the barby!**

*Lloyd Christmas unsuccessfully
sweet–talks an Austrian beauty*

# Young Frankenstein

**(1974) 108m PG**
Gene Wilder, Peter Boyle, Marty Feldman, Madeline Kahn, Cloris Leachman,
Teri Garr, Kenneth Mars, Richard Haydn, Gene Hackman
**D:** Mel Brooks
**S:** Gene Wilder, Mel Brooks

Brooks brings the moribund horror classic to exuberant black and white life, sparing no cliche. Young Dr. Frankenstein (Wilder, at his manic best), a successful American medical professor, inherits the old homestead back in Transylvania. He finds the locals just as grumpy about his family's history as he is, leaving only his snooty fiancée (Kahn), hunchbacked assistant Igor (pronounced eye–gore), spooky old hag Frau Blucher (Leachman), and a beautiful young fraulein (Garr) as allies. Clearly, Frankenstein ("That's Franken-steen") needs to make a friend. So he does, literally. Once he discovers old grandad's diaries, it's off to the graveyard for some spare parts. The monster (Boyle) has the body of a rather large killer, and is supposed to have the brain of a renowned scientist. Igor's confusion at the lab while pilfering the brain causes the monster to have a somewhat different personality. (Frankenstein: "What was the name on the jar?" Igor: "Abby something, I think. Abby Normal.") Despite this setback, the Doc manages to turn him into a song–and–dance man (they perform a rousing duet to Irving Berlin's "Puttin' On the Ritz") until fire, which we all know is bad, mucks up the works, sending the monster on a rampage. While on his rampage, the monster meets a little girl, a blind man (Hackman) with a fondness for cigars, and the future Mrs. Frankenstein, who he proceeds to deflower ("Oh sweet mystery of life, at last I've found you!"). The townspeople, led by the prosthetically enhanced police chief (Mars), decide to destroy the monster, leaving Dr. Frankenstein no choice but to give Frankie Big Shoes some of his own brain juice. The monster, in return, sends something the Doc's way that makes him very popular among the ladies. Writers Brooks and Wilder lay on the one–liners ("What knockers!" "Oh, sank you!"), while Leachman ("He vass my-boyfriend!") and

*Dr. Frankenstein serenades his captive audience.*

Feldman ("Call it-a hunch, ba–da–boom") are perfect as the old–world sidekicks. Brooks stays behind the camera for this one, which is widely held as his best work. Coincidence? You be the judge.

## Sed–a–give! Give him a sed–a–give!

*Igor guesses wrong on
Dr. Frankenstein's frantic charades clues*

# The Naked Gun: From the Files of Police Squad!

**(1988) 85m PG-13**

Leslie Nielsen, Ricardo Montalban, Priscilla Presley, George Kennedy,
O.J. Simpson, Susan Beaubian, Nancy Marchand, John Houseman;
**Cameos:** Dr. Joyce Brothers, Reggie Jackson, Weird Al Yankovic
**D:** David Zucker
**P:** Jim Abrahams, David Zucker, Jerry Zucker, Robert K. Weiss
**C:** Robert M. Stevens
**S:** Jim Abrahams, Pat Proft, David Zucker, Jerry Zucker
**M:** Ira Newborn

Police parody hilarity is the law for dim-bulb Lt. Frank Drebin in the *Naked Gun* trilogy, which crowned Nielsen the high priest of lowbrow. The first (and only) *Naked Gun* flick created by the entire ZAZ team is by far the best of the bunch, chock full of sight gags, puns, pratfalls, and too many cameos to catch the first time through; if important people in your life begin to complain about your obsessive film viewing, explain that *Naked Gun* must be watched over and over for the full mesmerizing effect. They'll understand. If not, write us, and we'll explain. Non-stop lunacy ensues when Drebin and Presley (in a move that surely sent the King spinning, before his daughter really gave him a twirl), the surprisingly goofy Kennedy, and O.J. (before, well, you know) team up to investigate a drug smuggler and protect the Queen of England from assassination. Two obligatory follow-ups, *The Naked Gun 2½: The Smell of Fear* and *The Naked Gun 33⅓: The Final Insult* pale a bit, but are still worth a look for those who like their laughs straight, no chaser. Diehards will want to check out *Police Squad!*, the short-lived, under-appreciated television show on which the series is based.

*Lt. Frank Drebin plays with his shadow.*

# Monty Python and the Holy Grail

**(1975) 90m PG**

Graham Chapman, John Cleese, Terry Gilliam, Eric Idle, Terry Jones,
Michael Palin, Carol Cleveland, Connie Booth, Neil Innes, Patsy Kensit
**D:** Terry Gilliam, Terry Jones
**P:** Mark Forstater, John Goldstone, Ralph the Wonder Llama
**C:** Terry Bedford
**S:** Graham Chapman, John Cleese, Terry Gilliam, Eric Idle, Terry Jones,
Michael Palin
**M:** Dewolfe, Neil Innes

And now for something completely different. The top 10 wouldn't be complete without the number 10, here worn by the Python troupe for their brilliant mistelling of the fabled Arthurian legend. Life in the Middle Ages ain't all it was cracked up to be, with belligerent peasants, filthy conditions, and a distinct lack of horses. *Holy Grail* opens in its own non-epic, low–budget manner; after the strangely near-Swedish subtitled credits, a horse is heard galloping toward the castle wall, and is revealed to be King Arthur (Chapman) on foot, followed by his loyal servant Patsy (Gilliam) banging coconut shells for equine sound effects. There's more singing and dancing knights who lack horses, foul-mouthed French taunters ("I fart in your direction, your mother was a hamster, and your father smelled of elderberries"), leftist peasants, shrubberies, blood-thirsty rodents, more shrubberies, and a Trojan rabbit. What else can you expect when the wisest mystic in all the land (ala Merlin) is called Tim? Jam-packed full of loony characters like the word-a-phobic knights who say "Nee" (they can't stand to hear the word "it") and an utterly dis-membered but extremely feisty Black Knight, who begs to dis-agree when informed that his appendages are being severed one by one during his sword fight with Arthur. Camelot is indeed a silly place.

*"We are the knights from Camelot. We eat ham and jam and Spam a lot."*

## From the book adapted for the film

The wise sir Bedevere was the first to join King Arthur's knights.
But other illustrious names were soon to follow. Sir Lancelot, the
Brave. Sir Galahad, the Pure. Sir Robin, the Not-Quite-So-Brave-
As-Sir-Lancelot, who had nearly fought the Dragon of Angnor; who
had nearly stood up to the vicious Chicken of Bristol; and who had
personally wet himself in the Battle of Badon Hill. And the aptly
named Sir Not-Appearing-In-This-Film. Together they formed a
band whose names and deeds were to be retold throughout the
centuries. The Knights of the Round Table.

# Sleeper

**(1973) 88m PG**
Woody Allen, Diane Keaton, John Beck, Howard Cosell,
Mary Gregory, Don Keefer, John McLiam
**D:** Woody Allen
**P:** Marshall Brickman, Jack Grossberg, Charles H. Joffe
**C:** David W. Walsh
**S:** Woody Allen, Marshall Brickman
**M:** Woody Allen, New Orleans Funeral Ragtime Orchestra,
Preservation Hall Jazz Band

Signature angst-ridden Allen, with a healthy dose of very silly slapstick thrown in, *Sleeper* is the tale of a future where candy bars are good for you and thoughts are controlled by the government. Neurotic Greenwich Village jazz musician/health food store owner Miles Monroe is put into deep freeze when an ulcer operation fails in 1973. Wrapped in aluminum foil, he awakes 200 years later to find himself enlisted in the battle to help overthrow leader Big Brother, who happens to be just a nose. That's right, no body. In fact, Big Brother's aides are planning to recycle his used tissues to clone a new order. Miles leaves the hospital disguised as a domestic robot and is delivered to upper–crust airhead Luna (Keaton), who has ordered him for her home. They become friends, and eventually (after much heated pseudo-intellectual discussion) she joins his revolutionary quest. Adapting to this strange new world poses problems for Miles; sex (the way Miles remembers it) is forbidden. Instead, people either rub a metal ball (The Orb) or climb into a booth-like contraption called "The Orgasmatron." Hilarious and highly inventive science fiction parody has a romping Dixieland score, giant vegetables, chase scenes, and even a Volkswagen joke.

*Woody doing his imitation of The Great Pumpkin*

# The Pink Panther

**(1964) 113m**
Peter Sellers, David Niven, Robert Wagner,
Claudia Cardinale, Capucine, Brenda de Banzie
**D:** Blake Edwards
**P:** Martin Jurow
**C:** Philip H. Lathrop
**S:** Blake Edwards
**M:** Henry Mancini

Bumbling inspector Clouseau is the primary reason this movie gets the *Idiot's* nod. A slick slapstick, *Panther* succeeds solely on the strength of Sellers' classic portrayal of the idiotic inspector. Disaster-prone, generally clueless, and the owner of a magnificently silly French accent, Clouseau succeeds in spite of himself. Switzerland may never recover when Clouseau invades a ski resort, obsessed with capturing a beyond-suave jewel thief (Niven) who's hoping to lift the priceless "Pink Panther" diamond. What the unsuspecting inspector doesn't know is that said thief is also his wife's lover; his wife clues Niven in on every move he makes. Laughs are guaranteed as the inspector stays hot on the trail of the elusive thief. Followed that same year by another *Panther* gem, *A Shot in the Dark*, starring Sellers and Elke Sommer and adapted from a French play aptly titled *L'Idiote*. It also marked the debut of over-enthusiastic judo instructor Kato (Burt Kwouk), who literally jumps in and thwarts the inspector's attempts to romance his blond co-star. The series was revived in 1975 with *The Return of the Pink Panther*, followed by a string of Sellers and post–Sellers sequels. Features one of the most recognizable theme songs in movie history, courtesy of Henry Mancini.

*Sellers as Clouseau is hot on the trail.*

## In the Pink with Sellers

Trail of the Pink Panther
(1982)

The Pink Panther Strikes
Again (1976)

Revenge of the Pink Panther
(1978)

Return of the Pink Panther
(1974)

A Shot in the Dark (1964)

THE 100 DUMBEST MOVIES OF ALL TIME

# Pee Wee's
# Big Adventure

**(1985) 92m PG**
Paul "Pee Wee Herman" Reubens, Elizabeth Daily, Mark Holton,
Diane Salinger, Judd Owen, Jan Hooks, Morgan Fairchild, James Brolin
**D:** Tim Burton
**P:** Richard Gilbert Abramson, Robert Shapiro
**C:** Victor J. Kemper
**S:** Phil Hartman, Paul Reubens, Michael Varhol
**M:** Danny Elfman

Not many candidates rode onto the dumb movie list on a bicycle. But then again, not many movies have Pee Wee. Some clever nasty has shaken up the tranquil but cartoonish world of the child-like hero. Pee Wee's beloved bike is missing, and the most likely candidate for the dastardly bike-napping is equally child-ish, snotty, rich neighbor Holton. But with no help from the authorities, Pee Wee consults a fortune teller, who tells him to search the basement of the Alamo. Plenty of laughs (Heh! Heh!) and zany adventures are in store for Pee Wee as he races to Texas, stumbling on a host of wacky characters along the way, such as spooky trucker "Large Marge" and a biker gang that he tames with a lively but bizarre dance routine performed to the tune of "Tequila" (take note of the platform shoes he borrows for this entertaining stint). It's adventures galore as he hitchhikes across America and even saves some animals from a burning pet store ("Ewwwww, snakes!"). Wow, that's a pretty big adventure. But, wait, there's more. The entire time, he's being pursued by Daily, a bike store clerk who is smitten with Pee Wee, though he does not return the sentiment. All is well in the end and a Hollywood bigwig finds his story so phenomenal that he makes it a movie. Go figure.

*Pee Wee proudly displays his five o'clock shadow.*

# Duck Soup

**(1933) 70m**

Groucho Marx, Chico Marx, Harpo Marx, Zeppo Marx, Louis Calhern,
Margaret Dumont, Edgar Kennedy, Raquel Torres, Leonid Kinskey,
Charles Middleton
**D:** Leo McCarey
**P:** Herman Mankiewicz
**S:** Bert Kalmar, Harry Ruby, Arthur Sheekman, Nat Perrin

A classic comedy with a modern sensibility and highly influential among film folks trying their hand at wild slapstick, *Duck Soup* serves up comic anarchy in a short sustained burst of Marxian brilliance. Though a flop at the box office and the last Marx effort for Paramount, its legend has only grown through the years. Groucho becomes the dictator of Freedonia thanks to million-airess Dumont (who did seven films with the comic troupe) and decides to start a war with neighboring Sylvania for no apparent reason—except that he wants to (the rent was already paid on the battlefield).   He sends double–agents Chico and Harpo, dressed up like him, to steal war plans, and thus begins the famous mirror sequence.  Madcap craziness ensues, war breaks out, and the casualties mount, thanks mostly to Groucho, who shoots several of his own men. Zeppo plays a love–sick tenor, a role he had perfected, in this, his last film with the brothers.  At the time, Mussolini was so insulted by the slapstick depiction of a dictator that he banned the film in Italy, and so Italians lost an important opportunity to laugh and went to war instead. See it with Woody Allen's *Love and Death* for a full evening of inspired comic mayhem on the battlefield.

---

### Soup Talk

**Rufus:** I suggest we give him ten years in Leavenworth or eleven years in Twelveworth.

**Chicolini:** I tell you what I'll do. I'll take five and ten in Woolworth.

---

*The Marx Bros. ham it up.*

---

**More Marx Mayhem**

*Duis autem vel*

| | |
|---|---|
| A Night in Casablanca (1946) | Horse Feathers (1932) |
| A Day at the Races (1937) | Monkey Business (1931) |
| A Night at the Opera (1935) | Animal Crackers (1930) |

# Wayne's World

**(1992) 93m PG-13**

Mike Myers, Dana Carvey, Tia Carrere, Rob Lowe, Brian Doyle-Murray, Lara Flynn Boyle, Kurt Fuller, Colleen Camp, Donna Dixon, Ed O'Neill
**Cameos:** Alice Cooper, Meatloaf
**D:** Penelope Spheeris
**P:** Howard W. Koch Jr., Lorne Michaels
**C:** Theo Van de Sande
**S:** Mike Meyers, Bonnie Turner, Terry Turner
**M:** J. Peter Robinson

Destined to be compared with *Citizen Kane* and *Gone With the Wind* as one of the greatest films ever made-not! Well, no, it's not worthy. But *Wayne's World* does have a certain simplistic freshness, a sense of neo–absurdist comic timing, a minimalist approach to sassy teen humor, that captured the heart of the nation during the confused early years of the '90s. What started out as a spasmodic *Saturday Night Live* sketch about two crispy metalheads who broadcast a local cable show from their basement turned into one of the top grossing films of the year and made Myers a film star, a neat trick at that. It has all the right elements: unique dialogue with inventive words (hurl, schwing), beautiful babes (Carrere, Dixon) and Rob Lowe (boo, hiss) as a slimy producer out to commercialize the public access show. The "Bohemian Rhapsody" and "Grey Poupon" scenes are just two whimsical examples of the special, subtle amusement and innocence captured by *Beverly Hillbillies* director Spheeris. But ten years from now, will viewers return to this for rip–snorting laughs as they do to *Airplane*? Yes, we believe they will. For *Wayne's World* tells its slight story well, as the boys meet idol Alice Cooper, resist fame and fortune, and stay true to their cable roots. *WW*'s huge success spawned a sequel in 1993, in which Wayne and Garth create a major concert, Waynestock. Not up to the original's minimalistic standards, though the scene with the goofy pair singing "YMCA" with the Village People is a hoot.

*Wayne and Garth give Claudia Schiffer two, er, thumbs up.*

## Wayne and Garth discuss the mysteries of love

**Garth:** Wayne, what do you do if every time you see this one incredible woman, you think you're gonna hurl?

**Wayne:** I say hurl. If you blow chunks and she comes back, she's yours. If you spew and she bolts, it was never meant to be.

# Raising Arizona

**(1987) 94m PG-13**
Nicholas Cage, Holly Hunter, John Goodman,
William Forsythe, Randall "Tex" Cobb, Trey Wilson,
M. Emmet Walsh, Frances McDormand, Sam McMurray
**D:** Joel Coen
**P:** Ethan Cohen
**C:** Barry Sonnenfeld
**S:** Ethan Coen, Joel Coen
**M:** Carter Burwell

Excellent deadpan performances and a script loaded with hilariously vivid backwoods poetry win the *Idiot's* favor. Dumb as a stump but good-hearted petty crook H.I. "Hi" McDonnough (Cage) marries prison officer Edwina (Hunter) and moves to a trailer in the middle of the Arizona desert. They long for a normal family life, but Ed can't get pregnant ("Her insides were a rocky place where my seed could find no purchase"), and Hi's shady past makes adoption impossible. It just so happens that unpainted-furniture tycoon Nathan Arizona (Wilson) and his wife Polly's quintuplets are front-page news and quite a handful, so Hi and Ed decide to help themselves to one of the infants. The plotline begs for complications, which turn up when two of Hi's old cellmates, brothers Gale and Evelle, (Goodman and Forsythe) escape from prison and seek sanctuary with the young family. A thoroughly bizarre rabbit-shooting biker (Cobb) is hired by Arizona Senior to find his kidnapped quint. Cage adds a brilliant deadpan quality and likability to his redneck character, and Hunter's first starring film role is full of a fresh raucous energy that rises to a near-hysterical level of maternal anxiety. It's pretty clear why Hi must nab a baby. Cinematographer Barry Sonnenfeld, who graduated to directing *The Addams Family* adds a sense of bizzaro-world photographic adventure to the mix, highlighted by the wild chase involving stolen diapers. Stupid, but fully realized.

*Baby's first heist.*

**Gale:** All right, ya hayseeds, this is a stickup. Everybody freeze and get down on the ground.

**Old Man:** Well, which is it, young feller? You want I should freeze or get down on the ground? I mean to say if I freeze, I can't rightly drop, and if I drop, I reckon I'll be in motion.

*Gale and a customer discuss
the logistics of a bank robbery*

# Ace Ventura: Pet Detective

**(1993) 87m PG-13**
Jim Carrey, Dan Marino, Courtney Cox, Sean Young, Tone Loc,
Noble Willingham, Troy Evans, Randall "Tex" Cobb
**D:** Tom Shadyac
**P:** James G. Robinson
**C:** Julio Macat
**S:** Jack Bernstein, Jim Carrey, Tom Shadyac
**M:** Ira Newborn

Most critics thought this one was likely to be gone and quickly forgotten, a stupid and scatalogical pet detective yarn that clearly showed the bake-sale budget and local-access skills of the filmmakers. It was hard to compare it to other pet detective yarns (like the box says, "he's the only one there is"), and Carrey, mostly a geeky regular on Fox TV's *In Living Color*, seemed an acquired taste at best. But then *Ace*, with its onslaught of mostly dumb situations endured by Carrey while doing postmodern Jerry Lewis on speed, was adopted by the wealthy, taste–making adolescents of America, bringing enormous box office success to the most surprised studio in Hollywood. And it became a career maker for Carrey, who's now rumored to be the $20 million man (our greatest fear is that he'll be tempted to show his range by doing Shakespeare). It's not a B–movie; it's a B–event. So maybe the critics learned a thing or two, like don't dis movies just cause they're rendering a stupid story about a pet detective. Not when they feature a comedian with morphing potential. Allllllllrighty, then. Ventura may not "do human," but humans dig him . . . all the way to the bank. A guilty pleasure for many, mainly because of Carrey's hyperactive portrayal of the pet dick who drops everything to find the Miami Dolphins' kidnapped mascot, Snowflake. Embracing the one-page plot narrative in a role he was meant to play, Carrey antagonizes his police adversaries (particularly Young, perfectly cast again as a near–human) and uses his canine abilities to foil the bad guys/gals and save the dolphin. Along the way, he makes you care. Plus there's Cox before

*Jim Carrey and "jungle friend."*

*Friends,* making this a memorable cinematic experience right up there with rewinding *The Godfather*. *Ace Ventura* creates a mania and language all his own, and since it's mostly on a grade–school level, we're proud to add it to the *Idiot's* list. Look for the sequel, *Ace Ventura: When Nature Calls.*

# The Nutty Professor

**(1963) 107m**
Jerry Lewis, Stella Stevens, Howard Morris, Kathleen Freeman, Del Moore,
Med Flory, Howard Morris, Elvia Allman, Henry Gibson
**D:** Jerry Lewis
**P:** Ernest D. Gluckman
**C:** W. Wallace Kelley
**S:** Jerry Lewis, Bill Richmond
**M:** Walter Scharf

Lewis, the toast of Paree and currently enjoying a career renaissance on Broadway in *Damn Yankees*, swings for the fences in what is arguably the best film of his career, which he co–wrote in addition to starring, directing, and co–producing (the man likes control). There's a near–heartfelt message: you might as well be yourself, because being someone else is too time consuming. This may seem ironic coming from a man with several personalities, but remember that without Jerry Lewis, Jim Carrey would be much different, and without *The Nutty Professor*, *The Mask* would still be looking for inspiration. Lewis is great as geeky, algaenous science professor Kelp, who seeks to move up the food chain in order to capture the heart of the most popular girl in class (Stevens). That's quite a task, so he puts his chemicals where his mouth is and creates a magical potion that transforms him into a suave playboy. Problem is, the mixture has an annoying way of wearing off at inconvenient times and more than once, he flees Cinderella-like (or rather, *Cinderfella*-like) to the safety of his lab. Lighthearted Jekyll and Hyde parody showcases Lewis at his zany best as the buck-toothed Kelp and foreshadows his incarnation as playboy Buddy Love, overbearing and narcissistic, but irresistable to women nonetheless. Many smell a spoof (or is that Brylcreem?) of Lewis' longtime partner Dean Martin when they watch this one, though Lewis diplomatically denies it. On the other hand, Buddy does bear a certain resemblance to the older telethon Jerry.

*Oui love you, Jerry!*

## Jerry's Vids

The Bellboy (1960)

Cinderfella (1960)

Jumping Jacks (1952)

The Ladies' Man (1961)

The Patsy (1964)

The Road to Bali (1953)

# Strange Brew

**(1983) 91m PG**
Rick Moranis, Dave Thomas, Max von Sydow, Paul Dooley, Lynne Griffin;
*Voice of:* Mel Blanc
**D:** Rick Moranis, Dave Thomas
**C:** Steven B. Poster
**S:** Rick Moranis, Dave Thomas
**M:** Steve DeJarnatt

How's it goin', eh? Bob and Doug MacKenzie, the back bacon–eating, cruller–loving, toque–wearing, beer–worshiping brothers from the Great White North who introduced the world to the charms of Canadian life on *SCTV*, hit the big screen with the expected silly results. At a screening of their flick *The Mutants from 2051 A.D.* (filmed in 3-B-three beers), Bob and Doug get booed out of the theatre. In a fit of panic, they give a disgruntled audience member a ticket refund with their dad's beer money. Desperate, they try to scam a free case of beer with the old "mouse-in-a-bottle" trick and travel to Elsinore Brewery. There they stumble upon the world domination scheme of an evil brew master (von Sydow), who tests his special mind–control brew on inmates from the asylum next door (upon hearing organ music, the inmates become hockey-playing killing machines). Only Bob and Doug can stop the brew from being given to unsuspecting drinkers at Oktoberfest (with the help of their beer–drinking, skunk–striped flying dog, Hosehead). Surprisingly adventurous (complete with car chases, murder, a near–drowning in a beer vat, and a few mean cross checks), *Strange Brew* provides a tutorial on Canadian backwoods speak ("take off", "beauty," "soakers," "bonus," "hoser," "good day," and the multipurpose "eh?"), as well as a new appreciation for the powers of golden lager. Koo loo koo koo koo koo koo koo!

*The MacKenzie brothers sit down to a healthy breakfast.*

# I'm Gonna Git You Sucka

**(1988) 89m R**

Keenen Ivory Wayans, Bernie Casey, Steve James, Isaac Hayes, Jim Brown,
Ja'net DuBois, Anne–Marie Johnson, Antonio Fargas, Eve Plumb,
John Vernon, Clu Gulager, Kadeem Hardison, Damon Wayans, Gary Owens,
Clarence Williams III, David Alan Grier, Kim Wayans, Robin Harris,
Chris Rock, Dawnn Lewis, Jester Hairston;
**Cameos:** Robert Townsend
**D:** Keenen Ivory Wayans
**P:** Carl Craig, Peter McCarthy
**C:** Tom Richmond
**S:** Keenen Ivory Wayans
**M:** David Frank

Given our fondness for poor spelling, *Git* is by title alone deserv-
ing of mention. The setting, Any Ghetto, U.S.A., is just the first
clue that viewers are in for urban spoof and slapstick,
Wayans–style. Writer, director and star Keenen Ivory Wayans,
along with brother Damon, lead a cast comprised of the top "blaxploitation" actors of the '70s, including Bernie Casey (*Hit Man*,
1972), Isaac Hayes (1974's *Truck Turner*) and Jim Brown, of
*Slaughter* (1972) fame. As with most spoofs, the stereotypes are
the prime target and with characters named Jack Spade, Slade,
Flyguy, Hammer, Slammer, and the token white bad guy, Mr. Big
(Vernon), *Sucka* is no exception. The movie follows Spade (Keenen Ivory), who returns home from a military tour of desk and
latrine duty for his brother June Bug's funeral. He learns that
June Bug was mixed up with the wrong crowd and died at the
hands of the scourge of the inner–city, death by "O.G" (over–gold,
i.e. too many gold chains). He seeks out Jack Slade (Casey), a
Shaft-like character now retired to running inner-city gang ath-
letic events like competitive car stripping, sack races where the
participants carry televisions on their shoulders and are chased
by dogs, and a senior citizen mugging contest. With Slade's
reluctant help, Spade recruits two more aging crime–fighters-
Hayes and Brown spoofing the characters they made famous dur-

*Just the boys from the band in 'Sucka.'*

ing the heyday of "blaxploitation" movies—to rid the streets of gold–pushers. Armed to the teeth, they totter off to battle. Slade even has his own band of musicians following him, playing the "Theme from Shaft," a tune written by Hayes ("That's my theme music" he explains. "Every good hero should have some!"). With a nod to *Airplane!* and Mel Brooks, Wayans delivers a gag at every opportunity. Classic is Fargas' pimp, who emerges from prison resplendid in *Superfly* threads, including giant platform heels with goldfish floating in them. *The Mod Squad*'s Clarence Williams III has a cameo as a '60s radical hopelessly out of touch with the times, while Plumb is his Brady-like wife. *Rambo* and *The Exorcist* also are spoofed in passing. The best Keenen Ivory flick for sure.

THE 100 DUMBEST MOVIES OF ALL TIME

# Fast Times at Ridgemont High

**(1982) 116m R**
Sean Penn, Jennifer Jason Leigh, Judge Reinhold, Robert Romanus,
Brian Backer, Phoebe Cates, Ray Walston, Scott Thompson,
Vincent Schiavelli, Amanda Wyss, Forest Whitaker, Kelli Maroney, Eric
Stoltz, Pamela Springsteen, James Russo, Martin Brest, Anthony Edwards
**D:** Amy Heckerling
**P:** Irving Azoff, Art Linson
**C:** Matthew F. Leonetti
**S:** Cameron Crowe, based on his novel

Based on Cameron Crowe's investigative study of hormonal teens trapped in high school, this cult fave was, like, one of the best adolescent sexploitation movies to come out of the '80s and bears more than a passing resemblance to *American Grafitti* for the sheer number of young actors it showcased. The rituals of dating and mating are prodded and probed as a year in the life of a group of teenagers is explored in detail (usually at the mall). Extremely horny but inexperienced waitress Stacy (Leigh) desperately wants to "cure" her virginity, so she asks more worldly co-worker Linda (Cates) for advice. She then practices fellatio on a carrot and discovers that sex is more complicated than a simple romp in the hay or the dugout or the swimming pool. Meanwhile, Stacy's brother Brad (Reinhold) is dealing with his own sexual frustrations, not to mention job troubles, which reach their climax when he's discovered masturbating by Cates. Usual school stereotypes make an appearance, including the nice homely guy (Backer as Mark Ratner) the hustler (Romanus as Mike Damone), and the guy who's never gonna graduate: a bitchin' Spicoli (Penn) as a stoned surfer dude. Forefather of Bill, Ted and Garth,  Spicoli sums up American history for teacher Mr. Hand (Walston, in a standout role as the teacher we all tried to avoid in high school): "So this Jefferson dude says, 'We just left England cuz it was bogus, so if we don't get some cool rules pronto, we'll just be bogus too.'" Look for film debutantes Edwards and Stoltz spilling out of Spicoli's smoking van as the

*Sean Penn as the unparalled surfer prototype.*

stoner buds, director Brest as a morgue doctor, and Nicolas Coppola (later Cage, in his first role) as a buddy of Brad's. Another debut worth noting: Whitaker as Ridgemont's menacing football ace who single–handedly takes out the Lincoln High team. Director Heckerling manages to apply a female perspective to the teenage hijinks formula by putting women characters in the spotlight and using the boys as amusing hood ornaments. Cool '80s soundtrack contributed by likes of Joe Walsh, The Go–Gos, Jimmy Buffet, The Cars, Poco, and Don Henley. See it with *Dazed and Confused*, and be glad you've escaped adolescence.

# Blazing Saddles

**(1974) 90m R**
Cleavon Little, Harvey Korman, Madeline Kahn, Gene Wilder, Mel Brooks,
John Hillerman, Alex Karras, Dom DeLuise, Liam Dunn
**D:** Mel Brooks
**P:** Michael Herzberg
**C:** Joseph F. Biroc
**S:** Andrew Bergman, Mel Brooks, Richard Pryor, Norman Steinberg,  Alan Uger
**M:** John Morris

Measured by the beans around the campfire flatulence scene alone, Brooks' classic western spoof deserves mention, though certainly group flatulence alone is not enough for such an eminent position on the list. Always less than subtle with satiric jabs, Brooks gleefully lays it on thick with wacky humor, yards of slapstick, and the obligatory skewer of every last cliche in the western genre. It was a movie waiting to happen and a cult happening in its early years, with prolonged showing on the midnight cinema circuit. Black (literally) Bart (Little) is hired as sheriff of the town of Rock Ridge in the hopes that the prejudiced citizens will panic and sell their land to crooked speculators. When the townsfolk turn on him because, for one thing, he's black, he's forced to call on the jail's only con, Jim the Waco Kid (Wilder), once the terror of the West and now a washed-up boozer. With a cast chock full of comedy greats, including Kahn in a classic takeoff of Marlene Dietrich's saloon belles and Korman as crooked Attorney General Hedley Lamarr, *Blazing* saddles loony characters with an abundance of Brooksian humor. Among the most vicious criminals in the West are Hell's Angels, Ku Klux Klansmen, Nazi storm troopers, Arab terrorists, and Alex Karras as the brute, Mongo. Hard to believe, but Brooks made both *Blazing Saddles* and *Young Frankenstein*, his great spoof of monster movies, in the same year.

*Mel goes native as a half–Jewish Indian.*

| Brooksian Brilliance | Mediocre Mel |
| --- | --- |
| High Anxiety (1977) | Robin Hood: Men in Tights (1993) |
| Young Frankenstein (1974) | |
| The Producers (1968) | Spaceballs (1987) |

# Polyester

**(1981) 86m R**
Divine, Tab Hunter, Edith Massey, Mink Stole, Stiv Bators, David Samson,
Mary Garlington, Kenneth King, Joni-Ruth White
**D:** John Waters
**P:** John Waters
**C:** David Insley
**S:** John Waters
**M:** Michael Kamen

Who could resist a film that caters to the viewers' olfactory pleasures? Think about watching this one with an "Odorama" card, which contains scratch-n-sniff scents corresponding to specific scenes and was given to original movie-goers. Moronic satire of middle-class life has hopelessly pathetic Baltimore housewife Divine dealing (not so well) with family problems while pining for the man of her dreams (played by 1950s heartthrob Hunter). A cheating husband, contemptuous disco-queen daughter, sexually frustrated (to say the least) son, and suicidal dog cause Divine to turn to the most attractive alternative—the bottle. Watch for King as Divine's hilariously disturbed son. Having Divine for a mother is enough to give any male problems, but this child is particularly screwed up—he spends his free time sniffing glue and getting his sexual kicks from stomping on women's feet in public. Waters' first mainstream film has bad taste written all over it. But that's the point.

*Divine with the man and horse of her dreams.*

> **B**oBo's dead, and I had a miscarriage.
> **But I discovered macrame.**
>
> *Mary Garlington, as Lulu Fishpan, lost her*
> *boyfriend but found solace in her art*

# Hot Shots!

**(1991) 83m PG-13**
Charlie Sheen, Cary Elwes, Valeria Golino, Lloyd Bridges, Kevin Dunn, Jon
Cryer, Kristy Swanson, William O'Leary
**D:** Jim Abrahams
**P:** Bill Badalato
**C:** Bill Butler
**S:** Jim Abrahams, Pat Proft
**M:** Sylvester Levay

Yet another spoof from some of the same folks who brought us
*Airplane!* and *The Naked Gun. Hot Shots!* is a wicked sendup of
*Top Gun* and other flyboy epics, but the parody doesn't stop
there. Attacking everything from *9½ Weeks* and *Diner* to *The
Fabulous Baker Boys* and *Dances with Wolves*, nothing is sacred.
Sheen is perfectly cast as Topper, a pilot whose mission is to
avenge his father's honor-and save the world at the same time.
Other air corps buddies include Elwes as Topper's chief rival,
Cryer as Washout, O'Leary as Dead Meat, and so on. Tons of sight
gags guarantee laughs that don't require much thought, and if
one doesn't work (and a lot of them don't), another is due in sec-
onds. Sheen gained a whole new career in comedy (a timely
occurrence), as he seems to understand that his main goal is not
necessarily to be funny, but rather to spoof himself, particularly
his role in 1990's *Navy SEALs*. Followed by the equally moronic
*Hot Shots! Part Deux*, a game spoof of the *Rambo* flicks and
other mindless adventure films.

## Dances with bikers got this for you.

*Topper receives a parting gift from his
Native American friends during
a spoof of "Dances with Wolves."*

*Ramboesque Charlie Sheen*

# The Blues Brothers

**(1980) 133m R**
Dan Aykroyd, John Belushi, James Brown, Cab Calloway, Ray Charles,
Henry Gibson, Aretha Franklin, Carrie Fisher, John Candy, Murphy Dunne,
Steve Cropper, Donald "Duck" Dunn, Matt "Guitar" Murphy;
**Cameos:** Frank Oz, Steven Spielberg, Twiggy, Paul "Pee Wee Herman"
Reubens, Steve Lawrence, John Lee Hooker
**D:** John Landis
**P:** Robert K. Weiss, Bernie Brillstein
**C:** Stephen M. Katz
**S:** Dan Aykroyd, John Landis
**M:** Elmer Bernstein, Ira Newborn

Crash! Boom! Screech! Get out of their way, 'cause they're on a
mission from God. Yes, those hoodlums of rhythm and blue-eyed
soul have crashed onto the dummy list. Aykroyd and Belushi are
Jake and Elwood Blues, orphaned blues singers who have been
deemed the chosen ones to raise money for the orphanage where
they spent their youth. In their quest to round up members from
their defunct band (which looks suspiciously like Booker T's) for
a concert reunion, Jake and Elwood run rampant in the streets
of Chicago, causing major car chases and crashes. Their total
disregard for the law and what little of a script there is give the
film and characters a deranged coolness. Full of action and soul-
ful cameos by Aretha Franklin, James Brown, and Cab Calloway,
*The Blues Brothers* is a mindless exercise in excess, but it has its
moments, including the boys belting out a sincere "Stand by
Your Man" in a redneck bar. Other tunes include "Think," "Boom
Boom," "Shake a Tail Feather," "Minnie the Moocher," "Everybody Needs Somebody to Love," "Sweet Home Chicago," "Jail-
house Rock," "Gimme Some Lovin'," and "The Theme from
Rawhide." Because of the heavy abundance of motor vehicle
destruction, the budget rose to $33 million, an astounding price
tag for a musical comedy back in 1980, especially since audi-
ences initially stayed away from it. A cult following developed,
and *The Blues Brothers* eventually blazed the trail for other big
screen *Saturday Night Live* sketches. The brothers blue also
show up for a quick cameo in *Roadie* (1980).

*The Blues Brothers pay a visit to Sister Mary Stigmata
at their childhood orphanage.*

**Elwood:** It's 106 miles to Chicago. We have a full tank of gas, half
    a pack of cigarettes, it's dark out, and we're wearing
    sunglasses.
**Jake:** Hit it.

# Fletch

**(1985) 98m PG**
Chevy Chase, Tim Matheson, Joe Don Baker, Dana Wheeler-Nicholson,
M. Emmet Walsh, Geena Davis, George Wendt, Alison La Placa
**D:** Michael Ritchie
**P:** Peter Douglas, Alan Greisman
**C:** Fred Schuler
**S:** Andrew Bergman, Gregory McDonald, based on his novel
**M:** Harold Faltermeyer

Chase gives the solo performance of his career in the title role as a resourceful investigative reporter doggedly in search of the big scoop. He provides nearly all of the laughs, and there's lots of them, as he impersonates a multitude of characters, including "Dr. Rosenpenis" and a guest at a country club who has a taste for Dom Perignon ("Put it on the Underhills' bill"). He diligently delves into the background of a suspicious corporate exec who hires Fletch to stage his murder, as he claims he has an incurable disease and wants his wife to collect the full insurance policy. The mystery unfolds as Fletch discovers that the executive is involved in crime with none other than the chief of police. Chase's rambling, sometimes muttered dialog delivered by his many different personas is especially funny, like when he's greeted at the door by a towel-clad woman ("My car just hit a water buffalo, can I borrow your towel?"). Look for Chevy sporting the biggest afro since *The Mod Squad* while he dreams of playing basketball with Kareem Abdul-Jabbar. Adapted from Gregory MacDonald's lightweight novel. Followed less successfully in 1989 by *Fletch Lives*, an event probably almost enjoyed by extremely ardent Chase fans.

> **You know, if you shoot me, you'll lose all those humanitarian awards.**
>
> *Fletch to bad guy Alan Stanwyk*

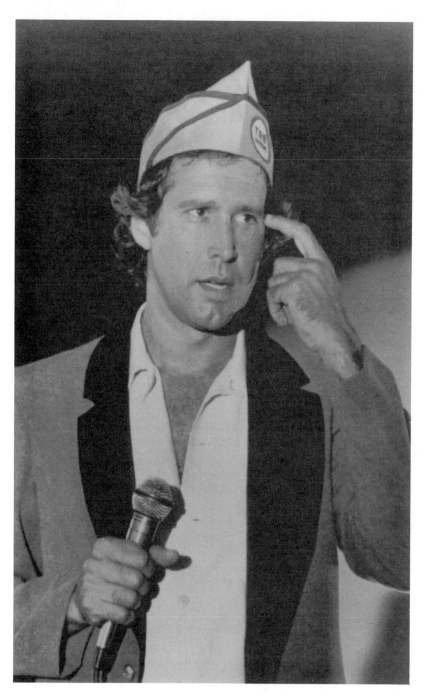

*Fletch: The master of disguise.*

# Up in Smoke

**(1978) 86m R**
Cheech Marin, Tommy Chong, Strother Martin, Edie Adams,
Stacy Keach, Tom Skerritt
**D:** Lou Adler
**P:** Lou Adler, Lou Lombardo
**C:** Gene Polito
**S:** Tommy Chong, Cheech Marin

Hey, like, mellow out, dude and let's take a look at what life was like before the PC and just-say-no police took over! Moronic forebears of *Dumb and Dumber,* Cheech and Chong made airhead fashionable in the '70s. A short trip in the wayback van reveals that the comedy team was huge during the Carter years, with a comedy act and records that worked that spacey repartee around the theme of recreational but illegal pharmaceuticals. The counterculture comedy duo hit the ultimate big time when they took their stoner shtick to the big screen with the first and best in a string of irreverent, crude comedies celebrating sex, drugs, rock and roll, and more drugs. Though only $2 million was spent on the film (but nobody can remember on what) and related paraphernalia, it became the most profitable movie released that year, and along with *Animal House* dominated the box office. Dated L.A. dope scene homage wraps every high-on cliché—the van, the cops, the parties, the munchies, the dead brain cells—around Cheech and Chong's trademark burnout banter. Somewhere in all this there may be a plot, which loosely follows C&C around town as they unwittingly (goes without saying) drive a van made out of marijuana. Meanwhile, obsessed officer Stedenko (Keach) is hot on their trail with his trio of incompetent cops. Skerritt does a bit as a crispy Vietnam vet with a bad birthmark on his face. While some of the drug scenes are hilarious, particularly those involving Chong's giant spliff, others showing the boys and their friends as drugged–out, barfing zombies seem fairly anti–drug; why would anyone want to do that? But it's Cheech and Chong; who cares? The one-liners alone make this one a worthwhile, albeit stupid, contact buzz.

*Uh oh! It's a bust!*

## Cheech and Chong: Numb & Number

Cheech and Chong's, The Corsican Brothers (1984)

Cheech and Chong's Nice Dreams (1981)

Cheech and Chong: Still Smokin' (1983)

Cheech and Chong's Next Movie (1980)

Cheech and Chong: Things Are Tough All Over (1982)

# Some Like It Hot

**(1959) 120m**
Marilyn Monroe, Tony Curtis, Jack Lemmon, George Raft,
Pat O'Brien, Edward G. Robinson
**D:** Billy Wilder, I.A.L. Diamond
**C:** Charles Lang, Jr.
**S:** Billy Wilder
**M:** Adolph Deutsch

A trio of lovely ladies, or rather one lovely lady and two guys impersonating lovely ladies, create a comedy classic. Curtis and Lemmon, two unemployed musicians, are in hot water with the mafia (or cold water if they end up thrown in the river) when they mistakenly witness the St. Valentine's Day massacre of 1929. They are forced to join an all-girl band (disguised as girls, of course) and flee from Chicago to the sunny safety of Miami, or so they think. Curtis falls for lead singer Monroe, but he must figure out a way to woo her without blowing his cover. Meanwhile, Lemmon is busy fighting off the advances of millionaire Brown, who has fallen in love with him. Plenty of hilarious fun until the mob convenes at the same hotel the "girls" are appearing at. Lemmon is convincing and comical in drag and Curtis is the perfect Cary Grant-type posing as a millionaire. But Brown has one of the most famous lines in film history; when spurned by Lemmon's marriage refusal and told he is actually a man, he quips, "Well, nobody's perfect." Interesting to note that the movie was filmed in black and white (much to the chagrin of Monroe, who preferred to be filmed in color) to hide the gaudy makeup required to disguise the men and make them appear to be believable as women. It worked.

> **We wouldn't be caught dead with men. Rough, hairy beasts. Eight hands. And they...they all want one thing from a girl.**
>
> *Jack Lemmon defends the "girls" position on dating.*

*You want some fries with that shake?*

# A Hard Day's Night

**(1964) 83m G**

John Lennon, Paul McCartney, George Harrison, Ringo Starr,
Wilfrid Brambell, Norman Rossington, Victor Spinetti, John Junkin,
Deryck Guyler, Anna Quayle, Kenneth Haigh, Richard Vernon, Eddie Malin,
Robin Ray, Lionel Blair, Alison Sebohm, Marrianne Stone, David Langton,
David Jaxon, Clare Kelly, Michael Trubshawe
**P:** Walter Shenson
**D:** Richard Lester
**W:** Alun Owen
**M:** John Lennon, Paul McCartney

Easily the best, most entertaining film of the three starring the
Beatles, despite (or because of) lack of a distinct plot, *Hard Day's*
takes us on a 36-hour musical/comedy ride with the lads from
Liverpool. The boys board a train to London, where they are
scheduled to do a TV show, with their Brian Epstein–like manager (Rossington), his assistant (Junkin), and Paul's fictitious
grandfather (Brambell) in tow. From the minute they arrive,
grandfather is stirring up trouble, and he flees his restrictive
grandson and his friends for a night of gambling and young
women. They track down the wanton senior and drag him back
to the hotel to rest up for the next day's gig at the studio. From
there on, the zany antics and visual gags, against a backdrop of
the appropriate musical accompaniment, take over, as production at the studio is delayed and grandpa is given more time to
cause anarchy and mayhem within the group. In what may have
been foreshadowing, the antiquated agitator takes Ringo aside
and, Yoko–like, suggests he's too good for the other members of
the band and should embark on a solo career, which the duped
Starr then sets out to do (see *Caveman*). Again, the boys are off
on the hunt, this time for their misguided drummer. Lester's use
of a variety of innovative film techniques, a very funny script,
and, of course, a great soundtrack make this an enduringly
amusing movie, one which succeeds apart from the popularity
and legacy of the Beatles. Songs include the title track, "Tell Me
Why," "I Should Have Known Better," "If I Fell," "And I Love
Her," "This Boy," and "Can't Buy Me Love."

# Attack of the Killer Tomatoes

**(1977) 87m PG**
David Miller, George Wilson, Sharon Taylor, Jack Riley,
Rock Peace, Eric Christmas
**D:** John De Bello
**P:** John De Bello, J. Stephen Peace
**C:** John K. Culley
**S:** John De Bello, Costa Dillon , Stephen Peace
**M:** Gordon Goodwin, Paul Sundfor

Climbing the vine is an intentionally saucy spoof of low-budget sci-fi and horror movies that tells the heartfelt story of giant tomatoes that suddenly become crazed attack fruit and terrorize the peaceful citizens of San Diego. Not your everyday garden-variety, these tomatoes are talented. For instance, they sing. The title, opening credits, and song parodies are the best parts of this campy romp, which coincidentally lacks anything resembling a plot. Then again, tomatoes in film are traditionally free spirits. The action begins as terrifying tomatoes do the killer shark bit from *Jaws*, bobbing at hapless, bikini–clad swimmers. Spoofing their way through parodies of traditional slasher flicks, the tomatoes eventually organize and conquer the country. But will the U.S. Army prove mightier than the humble tomato? Or perhaps, are the tomatoes merely pawns, juicy flunkies in a vicious game of evil? So suspects a mole in the tomato camp, who is found out as he inadvertently inquires for a highly controversial condiment amongst such company. The hilarious confrontation is not to be missed. For true fans of menacing fruit, don't stop here—race to your local video store to rent the sequels: *Return of the Killer Tomatoes* (bet George Clooney wishes he hadn't made this one now that he's the hotshot star of TV's *ER*!), *Killer Tomatoes Strike Back,* and *Killer Tomatoes Eat France.* It was even made into a TV cartoon. Laserdisc of *Killer T's* is now available, for those demanding tomatoes with finer resolution.

# Revenge of the Nerds

**(1984) 89m R**
Robert Carradine, Anthony Edwards, Timothy Busfield, Andrew Cassese,
Curtis Armstrong, Larry B. Scott, Brian Tochi, Julia Montgomery,
Michelle Meyrink, Ted McGinley, John Goodman, Bernie Casey
**D:** Jeff Kanew
**P:** Ted Field, Peter Samuelson
**C:** King Baggot
**S:** Jeff Buhai, Tim Metcalfe, Miguel Tejada–Flores, Steve Zacharias
**M:** Thomas Newman

Before Edwards hit it big as a slightly nerdy doctor on TV's *ER*, he played Gilbert, a really nerdy college freshman. Along with his good buddy Lewis (Carradine), Gilbert enters Adams College with dreams of being popular. They rush but are rejected by the frats as uncool and are forced to live in the gym. Kicked around and humiliated by the campus jocks and sexpot sorority babes, they take matters into their own weak and trembling hands by recruiting other campus geeks to start a branch of Lambda Lambda Lambda, an all-black frat. Continual harassment by the jock frat led by Stan the Man (McGinley) gets out of control, and the tri-Lams put their big-brained nerd heads together and plan sweet revenge. Carradine and Edwards pull off the stereotypical nerd facade to a tee, while Armstrong gives a memorable performance as the repulsively obscene nerd Booger (who does a pretty impressive belch). Moronic but funny feel-good satire (you'll be rooting for them nerds, though you'll feel ashamed afterward) is a cut above most other hijinks in college comedies and skewers the Greek system with glee. Followed in descending value by *Revenge of the Nerds 2: Nerds in Paradise* and the TV movie *Revenge of the Nerds 3: The Next Generation*, both of which push humorous nerdom beyond the tolerance level.

*Nerds receive ominous warning.*

**T**here are more of us than there are of them. Anyone who has ever felt excluded, left out, or unaccepted, whether you think you're a nerd or not—join us!

*Head nerd (Carradine) invites*
*fellow students to side with the nerds*

# Stripes

**(1981) 105m R**
Bill Murray, Harold Ramis, P.J. Soles, Warren Oates, John Candy,
John Larroquette, Judge Reinhold, Sean Young, Dave Thomas, Joe Flaherty
**D:** Ivan Reitman
**P:** Dan Goldberg, Ivan Reitman
**C:** Bill Butler
**S:** Len Blum, Dan Goldberg, Harold Ramis
**M:** Elmer Bernstein

To the tune of Manfred Mann's "Do Wah Ditty," an unlikely group of Army recruits march proudly onto the dummy list. This showcase of Second City players finds Murray and Ramis falling prey to the advertising world's depiction of the Army as some kind of Club Med. The two goof–ups enter the service with the expectation that boot camp is the answer to all their woes. Of course, the pair is thrown into a platoon of misfits and the basic training bumbling begins. Memorable scenes include the montage of hip drills performed by Murray and company on graduation day and Candy (who joined to lose weight) mud wrestling a gaggle of topless yet brutal babes during a night pass on the town. Oates adds to the fun as the grunting, hard-nosed drill sergeant Hulka, who is not phased at all by the casual anarchy that Murray and Ramis have created. Catch Murray at his wild best during a kitchen scene involving a pretty MP and various cooking utensils, and don't miss Larroquette as the moronic Capt. Stillman, who bears a resemblance to *Police Academy's* clueless Commandant Lassard. Hilarious ending involving a new fangled, top-secret armored truck disguised as a Winnebago.

*Bill Murray leads his motley crew.*

**W**e're Americans, with a capital "A." Do you know what that means? It means our forefathers were kicked out of every decent country in the world.

*John Winger (Murray), firing up the troops.*

# Gremlins 2:
# The New Batch

**(1990) 107m PG–13**
Phoebe Cates, Christoper Lee, John Glover, Zach Galligan;
**Cameos:** Jerry Goldsmith
**D:** Joe Dante
**P:** Michael Finnell, Kathleen Kennedy, Frank Marshall, Steven Spielberg
**C:** John Hora
**S:** Charles S. Haas
**M:** Jerry Goldsmith

While *Gremlins* spoofed the alien horror genre, *The New Batch* takes matters a surrealistic slapstick step or two further. The heroes of the original *Gremlins* are back again, as Billy (Galligan) and Kate (Cates) move to the big city to work for Donald Trump–like magnate Clamp. Clamp's evil plan to replace Chinatown with modern office buildings reunites Billy and Kate with their gremlin friend, now a test rabbit for Splice of Life lab's genetic experiments. One hilarious result is a singing gremlin who leads the others in a rousing chorus of "New York, New York." A sequel that is actually better than the original, *Gremlins 2* presents a less violent and far more campy vision of the future, paying myriad surreal tributes to scores of movies, including *The Wizard of Oz* and musical extravaganzas of the past. Set in a futuristic skyscraper in the Big Apple, director Dante makes elaborate use of high–tech special effects and sight gags to create a surface silliness masking a serious underlying theme: big business sucks, big media sucks, big medicine sucks, and new technology can really suck when left in the wrong hands. Rick Baker's gremlins are a dazzling, highly individualistic lot.

*Billy, Kate, and little Gizmo watch in horror as the cheerfully malevolent gremlins approach.*

**H**e reminds me of dolls hanging from suction cups staring out from behind car windows.

*-Villain John Glover referring to gremlin Gizmo*

# Monty Python's Life of Brian

**(1979) 60m**
Michael Palin, Graham Chapman, Eric Idle, John Cleese, Terry Jones,
Michael Palin, George Harrison
**D:** Terry Jones
**P:** John Goldstone, George Harrison
**C:** Peter Biziou
**S:** Graham Chapman, John Cleese, Terry Gilliam,
Eric Idle, Terry Jones, Michael Palin
**M:** Geoffrey Burgon

Well, it ain't no *Holy Grail*, but early Christianity is always good
for a few laughs. Following their quest for the grail, the Pythons
embark on this often riotous spoof of Christianity, tracking a
hapless peasant named Brian (Chapman) who is mistaken for the
messiah in 32 A.D. Worshipped by the prophet–loving peasants
and plagued by bumbling Roman soldiers, Brian stumbles from
one hilarious routine to the next and plays straight man to a
variety of characters, such as the vexed ex–leper Ben, whose
business has dropped off since being healed; Harry the Haggler,
who forces Brian to *lower* his bid for his wares, and the lisping
Pontius Pilate, played to the usual extreme by Palin. Brian manages to escape from Pilate as the latter is distracted by his own
soldiers who dare to laugh at the rather amusing names of
Pilate's friends (hint: exaggerated appendages). Eventually, however, the peasant is led to his ultimate fate, and only the most
pious will remain unamused at the chorus of crucifixion victims
who chirp "Always Look on the Bright Side of Life" while nailed
to their crosses.

*Brian's mother (Terry Jones) knows her son Brian (Graham Chapman) isn't the messiah, just a very naughty boy.*

**B**lessed are the cheesemakers.

*Jesus's followers misunderstand his Sermon on the Mount*

# National Lampoon's Vacations

## National Lampoon's Vacation

**(1983) 98m R**
Chevy Chase, Beverly D'Angelo, Imogene Coca, Randy Quaid,
Christie Brinkley, James Keach, Anthony Michael Hall, John Candy,
Eddie Bracken, Brian Doyle–Murray, Eugene Levy
**D:** Harold Ramis **P:** Matty Simmons **C:** Victor J. Kemper
**S:** John Hughes **M:** Ralph Burns

## National Lampoon's European Vacation

**(1985) 94m PG–13**
Chevy Chase, Beverly D'Angelo, Dana Hill, Jason Lively,
Victor Lanoux, John Astin
**D:** Amy Heckerling **W:** John Hughes, Robert Klane, Eric Idle **M:** Charles Fox

## National Lampoon's Christmas Vacation

**(1989) 93m PG–13**
Chevy Chase, Beverly D'Angelo, Randy Quaid, Diane Ladd, John Randolph,
E.G. Marshall, Doris Roberts, Julia Louis–Dreyfuss, Mae Questel,
William Hickey, Brian Doyle–Murray, Juliette Lewis, Johnny Galecki,
Nicholas Guest, Miriam FLynn
**D:** Jeremiah S. Chechik **W:** John Hughes **M:** Angelo Badalamenti

Dim-witted at its best moments, *National Lampoon's Vacation* proceeds religiously with its simple-minded theme: the family vacation from hell. Clark Griswold's (Chase) "quest for fun" means taking his family on a cross-country jaunt from their suburban Chicago home to the infamous "Walleyworld" amusement park (home of Marty Moose). The family piles into their metallic pea-green wagon queen family truckster (a gas-guzzling station wagon) to begin a precisely planned and timed, classic summer

*Chevy helps himself to a souvenir from Stonehenge.*

vacation. A visit with redneck relatives in Kansas and a quick look at the Grand Canyon are just two of the scheduled stops. But these are the Griswolds, so disaster develops at every turn, including an unexpected detour through the mean streets of St. Louis and a mishap with a bartender in the "Old West" tourist trap Dodge City. Morbidly memorable scenes include the untimely deaths of Aunt Edna and the family dog. Chase is a hoot as he races after dream girl Brinkley, falls asleep at the wheel, and threatens park security guard Candy. With this one under their belt, the Griswolds were not done traveling just yet. They receive a once-in-a-lifetime opportunity to reinforce the ugly American stereotype in *National Lampoon's European Vacation*. After winning a cut-rate economy ride through Europe on the game show "Pig in a Poke," the family endures mindless and sometimes hilarious travails, often with people who speak a different language. Far less mean-spirited than the first, but duller for the niceness. Even sillier (but better) is their stay-at-home holiday in *National Lampoon's Christmas Vacation*, where the simple-minded theme is the family holiday from hell.

# Back to School

**(1986) 96m PG-13**

Rodney Dangerfield, Keith Gordon, Robert Downey Jr., Sally Kellerman,
Burt Young, Paxton Whitehead, Adrienne Barbeau, M. Emmet Walsh,
Severn Darden, Ned Beatty, Sam Kinison, Kurt Vonnegut, Jr., Robert
Picardo, Terry Farrell, Edie McClurg, Jason Hervey
**D:** Alan Metter
**P:** Chuck Russell
**C:** Thomas E. Ackerman
**S:** Rodney Dangerfield, Steven Kampmann, William Porter, Harold Ramis,
Peter Torokvei
**M:** Danny Elfman

Rodney Dangerfield strings his trademark one–liners into a silly campus spoof that is perhaps best known for changing the drinking habits of his fans forever ("Bring a pitcher of beer every seven minutes till somebody passes out, and then bring one every ten minutes, alright?") Dangerfield is Thornton Melon, a self-made tall-and-fat clothing maven who dumps his shrewish wife (Barbeau) and enrolls in college to prove the value of education to his wimpy but good-natured son Jason (Gordon). While Jason struggles to make the diving team and win the heart of a beautiful co-ed (Farrell), Thornton becomes the hottest middle-aged guy on campus with his big spender, party hearty ways: he schmoozes Dean Martin (Beatty) with a fat donation, remodels his dorm digs into a luxury suite, joins a bar band onstage for a rousing rendition of "Twist and Shout," and snorkels in a hottub full of hot babes. He's not such a hit in the classroom, however, and he uses his cash to set up a homework brain trust (he even hires Kurt Vonnegut to write an English paper on Kurt Vonnegut). Conflict arises when Thornton falls for his English instructor (Kellerman). Her stuffy business professor boyfriend (Barbay) accuses Thornton of cheating and challenges him to pass his courses with oral exams or be expelled from school. Thornton also manages to help out the school's diving team during a crucial meet by performing his special dive, the "Triple Lindy." Definitely one of Dangerfield's best, ranking right behind *Caddyshack* on the short list. Includes the usual quiet perfor-

*Dangerfield commands respect from geeky co—eds.*

mance by Kinison as a Vietnam veteran history professor with no tolerance for revisionist theory.

**He really cares.
About what, I have no idea.**

*Thornton speaks of crazed history professor
played by Kinison.*

# Used Cars

**(1980) 113m R**
Kurt Russell, Jack Warden, Deborah Harmon,
Gerrit Graham, Joe Flaherty, Michael McKean, David L. Lander
**D:** Robert Zemeckis
**P:** Bob Gale
**C:** David Morgan
**S:** Bob Gale, Robert Zemeckis
**M:** Patrick Williams

The crude meter is in overdrive for this rowdy, raunchy tale of competing used car lots owned by rival brothers battling for business and access to a new freeway off ramp. Russell plays chief sales guy Rudy Russo, a slick charmer in loud plaid and polyester with political aspirations that necessitate a $50,000 payoff. When his boss Luke Fuchs (Warden) kicks off, Rudy and his fellow shysters hide the fact and the body from Fuchs' brother Roy (Warden, again) who wants to take over Luke's lot. Rudy, his superstitious sleazeball cohort Jeff (Graham), and their very large mechanic Jim (McRae) pirate advertising air time (once during a presidential address) with the help of McKean and Lander (that's Lenny and Squiggy to you) and host a disco stripper bonanza among their various hilarious stunts to get customers to cross the street from Roy's lot to theirs. When Luke's long lost daughter Barbara (Harmon) shows up in town and takes over the lot, the bunch faces the ultimate challenge: Get 250 used cars (a mile end–to–end) to the lot before a judge can declare them guilty of false advertising (it's a long story) and turn the lot over to Roy for good. Loads of cussing, fighting, bad suits, half–naked women, and high school sophomores convoying through the desert in cars from the Nixon administration fill in where the plot grinds to a halt. Russell's a riot, but the flick's best moments come from Graham: he guilts a family into buying a station wagon by making them think they ran over his dog (don't worry, PETA, it's only a rock under the tire), and he trashes a bar by spilling salt, breaking mirrors, opening umbrellas, and crawling under ladders in order to lose a bet on a football game.

*Lenny and Squiggy give fashion tips to used car salesmen Russell and Graham.*

**Mrs. Lopez, do you realize your hair matches the color of these tires?**

*Rudy Russo trying to score a sale*

# Slap Shot

**1977 123m R**

Paul Newman, Michael Ontkean, Jennifer Warren, Lindsay Crouse, Jerry
Houser, Andrew Duncan, Strother Martin, Jeff Carlson, Steve Carlson, David
Hanson, Melinda Dillon, M. Emmet Walsh, Swoozie Kurtz, Christopher
Murney, Paul Dooley
**D:** George Roy Hill
**P:** Stephen J. Friedman
**C:** Victor J. Kemper
**S:** Nancy Dowd
**M:** Elmer Bernstein

Newman reunites with Hill after *Butch Cassidy and the Sun-
dance Kid* and *The Sting* in this story of a ragtag hockey team
transformed into a crowd-pleasing powerhouse. Newman is Reggie Dunlop, 52 year-old player/coach of a minor league team in
Pennsylvania going nowhere. That is, until the players learn how
to break all the rules. Sort of a *Bad News Bears* for grownups,
with the usual ethical conflict (is it better to play clean and lose
or play dirty and win?), but with much more bleeding, swearing,
and confused sex. Coach Dunlop gathers an oddball mixture of
has–beens and neverwillbes and reluctantly teaches them the
ropes, using violence, mayhem, and the occasional cheap shot to
turn the team around. Ontkean, the star scorer, doesn't agree
with the new strategy, and at one point does a striptease on ice to
prove it. The most memorable part of the team-and the movie-
are the Hanson Brothers (Carlson, Carlson, and Hanson). This
trio of thick–spectacled misfits is hell on ice. Away from the
rink, they're peaceful and moronic, with an IQ of 60 and a shared
love for toy trucks; in uniform they're sociopaths on skates.
Infamous for its locker–room language, *Slap Shot* creatively uti-
lizes the full spectrum of four–letter words, serving as an effec-
tive primer for those learning English as a second language.
Scriptwriter Dowd claims it's all based on material gleaned from
tape recording her brother's stick–wielding cohorts; look for her
and brother Ned Dowd in bit parts.

*Coach Dunlop overflowing with enthusiasm while surveying his team's efforts.*

### It's a Fact

The "Hanson Brothers" still tour the country appearing at minor league hockey games and card shows.

# Ghostbusters

**(1984) 103m PG**
Bill Murray, Dan Aykroyd, Harold Ramis, Sigourney Weaver, Rick Moranis,
Annie Potts, Ernie Hudson, William Atherton
**D:** Ivan Reitman
**P:** Ivan Reitman
**C:** Laszlo Kovacs
**S:** Dan Aykroyd, Harold Ramis
**M:** Elmer Bernstein, Ray Parker, Jr.

Three scientists specializing in the paranormal go private enterprise with a ghost extermination business. The boys have great timing, as New York City is being overrun by spirits using an old apartment building as a gateway into our dimension. So who ya gonna call? Ray, Egon, and Peter (Aykroyd, Ramis, and Murray) soon encounter a resident (Weaver) of the building who thinks there might be trouble. Well, she's right, as hellhounds and a giant marshmallow man, aided by a pencil–pushing EPA geek (Atherton), soon demonstrate. Co–writers Aykroyd and Ramis are appropriately zany, but Murray, with his deadpan delivery and snide remarks, fires the best lines, and Moranis steals every scene he's in as a possessed accountant. Weaver's possession scene with Murray is a great advertisement for safe sex. Big–budget comedy (those giant marshmellow men cost money) drew $239 million at the box office, leading to the aptly named sequel *Ghostbusters 2*, in which the trio battle a spirit from a painting, a river of slime, and the sequel jinx, with varying degrees of success. As if a simple cassette was not enough, *Ghostbusters* is also available in laserdisc version with letter boxing, analysis of all special effects, complete screenplay and original trailer.

*Encountering some paranormal activity at the New York Public Library.*

**G**enerally you don't see that kind of
behavior in a major appliance.

*Dr. Venkman's reaction on
being told that a refrigerator
opened up to reveal a fiery, seething Hellscape*

# Clueless

**(1995) 133m PG–13**
Alicia Silverstone, Stacey Dash, Brittany Murphy, Paul Rudd, Dan Hedaya,
Donald Faison, Elisa Donovan
**D:** Amy Heckerling
**P:** Scott Rudin, Robert Lawrence
**C:** Bill Pope
**S:** Amy Heckerling, loosely based on the novel *Emma* by Jane Austen
**M:** David Kitay

An updated *Heathers* with a heart (and without the murderous subplot), *Clueless* tracks the shopping habits and fashion sense of Bronson Alcott High's very own "Bettys," Cher (Silverstone) and her friends, who "were named after great singers who now do infomercials." Cher, whose limited sphere of reference leads her to believe that she doesn't need to learn how to park, "since everywhere you go there's valet," is a spoiled but good–hearted teen trying hard to be more than just the most popular girl in school. She matches her outfits using a computer and yearns to makeover a frumpy teacher. Silverstone, first noticed as a Lolita–like psycho in *The Crush* and Aerosmith's video vixen, here plays a slightly more upscale character who charges her way through high school without a clue that there's cultural value outside Beverly Hills. If you find yourself saying, "Well, there isn't!" chances are you won't get most of the one–liners in the movie either, but for the rest of us, the preposterous excess and pop–culture of the "Y" generation is pretty amusing. Although *Clueless* at first glance seems totally culturally devoid—a "monet" is slang for someone who looks good from afar but is a mess up close and Hamlet is a guy played by Mel Gibson—it does have it's requisite share of literary references. Director Heckerling (*Fast Times at Ridgemont High*) pays tribute to female writers in the name of Cher's high school and even bases some of the plot on a Jane Austen novel, which proves you can successfully mix in a hint of a bygone era in a totally youth–oriented film where every high–schooler has a cellular phone to gossip on and a "postal" is a flipped–out whacko. As if. Hedaya is particularly

*Black–plumed Alicia Silverstone after a hard day at the mall.*

funny as Cher's humorless dad, a litigation lawyer (we know there's a redundancy there). Highlights that make this a natural for the top 100 include the scary freeway drive and Cher's aggressive but misguided matchmaking attempt at a party.

> **You see how picky I am about my shoes, and they go on my feet!**
>
> *-Cher on why she still is a virgin.*

# Top Secret!

**(1984) 90m PG**
Omar Sharif, Val Kilmer, Jeremy Kemp, Warren Clarke,
Peter Cushing, Lucy Gutteridge
**D:** David Zucker, Jim Abrahams, Jerry Zucker
**P:** Jon Davison, Hunt Lowry
**C:** Christopher Challis
**S:** Jim Abrahams, Martyn Burke, David Zucker, Jerry Zucker
**M:** Maurice Jarre

Silly farce from the creators of *Airplane!* navigates recklessly through spoofland, hitting and missing with equal aplomb. The ZAZ credentials alone are nearly enough to warrant status as one of the dumbest movies of all time, but *Top Secret!* has other merits as well. A parody of spy flicks and silly teen musicals (not an everyday combo), it features a pre-*Top Gun* Kilmer as Elvis-like rock singer Nick Rivers, whose hit single, "Skeet Surfin," ("When we shoot a curl, we really shoot a curl") has put him on the cover of *Rolling Stone* and *Guns and Bullets* magazines and made him a star. Touring East Germany as an official ambassador, he listens to German language tapes on the way to master key German phrases ("There is sauerkraut in my lederhosen; I want a schnauzer with my wiener schnitzel"). Once there, he falls in love with fraulein cutey Hillary (Gutteridge), whose name has an interesting origin, and helps her save her scientist dad from the hands of the evil Nazis, headed by an affable general whose official letterhead reads, "East Germany, Better Government Through Intimidation" and whose official stamp bears the mark: "Find him and kill him." American politics are satirized as well. Sez Hillary after noticing Nick is an American: "My uncle was born in America, but he was one of the lucky ones. He escaped in a balloon during the Jimmy Carter presidency." Song and dance numbers are highly amusing, like the funky waltz Nick and Hillary perform and Nick's own "Straighten the Rug." Skewers a number of popular films of the time, including a hilarious version of *Blue Lagoon*. Sophisticated it ain't, with very little plot, but never fear, those in search of cheap laughs will find plenty.

*Before "Batman Forever," Val Kilmer was actually an Elvis impersonator.*

As long as a single man is forced to cower under the iron fist of oppression, as long as a child cries out in the night, or an actor can be elected President, we must continue to struggle!

*Hillary, as she is held captive by the East Germans*

# Better Off Dead

**(1985) 97m PG**

John Cusack, Curtis Armstrong, Diane Franklin, Kim Darby, David Ogden
Stiers, Amanda Wyss, Curtis Armstrong, Vincent Schiavelli, Laura
Waterbury, Daniel Schneider, Aaron Dozier, Taylor Negron, Scooter Stevens
**D:** Steve Holland
**C:** Isidore Mankofsky
**S:** Steve Holland
**M:** Rupert Hines

To hell with the usual Brat Pack melodramas and horndog jiggle-
fests: any teen movie that includes a psychotic paperboy hellbent
on collecting two bucks, drag–racing Japanese brothers who
learned English from watching Howard Cosell, an evil ski expert
named Stalin, and an animated hamburger that lip–synchs Van
Halen's "Everybody Wants Some" deserves a spot on *Idiot's* list.
Lane Meyer (Cusack) is a typical high schooler who's obsessively
in love (to put it mildly) with his girlfriend Beth (Wyss)-but she
isn't quite so enthusiastic about him. After she dumps him for
Stalin (Dozier), the captain of the ski team, Lane's life goes into a
tailspin and he makes a few half–hearted but hilariously thwart-
ed attempts at ending his misery for good. His whacked–out family is no help either: hapless dad (Stiers) can't relate, mom
(Darby) is a complete loon (she gives frozen dinners as Christmas presents), and little brother Badger (get it?) is busy getting
mail order instructions on everything from picking up trashy
women to building a space shuttle from household appliances.
Cute French exchange student Monique (Franklin) moves in
with his obese, obnoxious neighbors and develops a crush on the
too-depressed-to-notice Lane. She helps him get his bitchin' '67
Camaro running and win a drag race against the tormenting
Cosell–inspired duo. His confidence bolstered, Lane manages to
ski down the most treacherous slope on the mountain (with the
paperboy in hot pursuit) and defeat the cheeseball Stalin. *Better
Off Dead* takes lots of quirky plot elements, sight gags, and the
occasional animated dream sequence that alone might be cause
for institutionalization and manages to link them together with
deadpan nuttiness. Director Holland was only 25 when he made
this flick, and thankfully it shows.

# Valley Girl

**(1983) 95 m R**
Nicolas Cage, Deborah Foreman, Colleen Camp, Frederic Forrest,
Michael Bowen, Cameron Dye
**D:** Martha Coolidge
**P:** Wayne Crawford, Andrew Lane
**C:** Frederick Elmes
**S:** Wayne Crawford, Andrew Lane
**M:** Marc Levinthal, Scott Wilk

Another direct predecessor to *Clueless*, this classic teen flick features the unlikely romance between Julie (Foreman), a deb from the Valley, and Randy (Cage), a punker from Hollywood. Although they're in love, Julie's tight–knit clique of friends doesn't approve of the leather crowd, which causes the suburbanite princess much distress. Like, totally. Cracking under peer pressure, Julie dumps Randy and goes back to ex–boyfriend Tommy, a dumb jock. Randy plots several ways in which to get her back, and the big confrontation turns into a hilarious night at the prom. Both of the leads do a great job, especially Cage as the rebel from "Hollyweird." Check out Julie's very liberal, ex–hippie parents for a few laughs. This funny, appealing story also features one of the best soundtracks ever recorded for a teen film, with songs by Modern English, Men at Work, The Plimsouls, Psychedelic Furs, Sparks, Josie Cotton, and others.

> **It's like I'm totally not in love with you anymore, Tommy—I mean, it's so boring.**
> *Julie dumps boyfriend Tommy for Randy*

# Young Woody

## Take the Money and Run

**(1969) 85m PG**
Woody Allen, Janet Margolin, Marcel Hillaire, Louise Lasser
**D:** Woody Allen
**P:** Charles H. Joffe
**C:** Lester Shorr
**S:** Woody Allen, Mickey Rose
**M:** Marvin Hamlisch

## Bananas

**(1971) 82m PG**
Woody Allen, Louise Lasser, Carlos Montalban, Howard Cosell,
Charlotte Rae, Conrad Bain;
**Cameos:** Sylvester Stallone, Allen (Gooritz) Garfield
**D:** Woody Allen
**S:** Woody Allen

Not typically known for the kind of humor found in lesser-evolved dumb flicks, Woody none the less injects a high level of no–holds–barred zaniness in his earlier films. *Take the Money and Run* was his high-speed directorial near-debut. Allen is Virgil Starkwell in this satirical documentary of the life of a bumbling criminal who begins his illustrious career by robbing vending machines. Hilarious one–liners and preposterous situations definitely make up for the sometimes uneven plot and direction.

> **I** robbed a butcher shop. I got away with 116 veal cutlets. Then I had to go out and rob a tremendous amount of breading.
>
> *Virgil in "Take the Money and Run"*

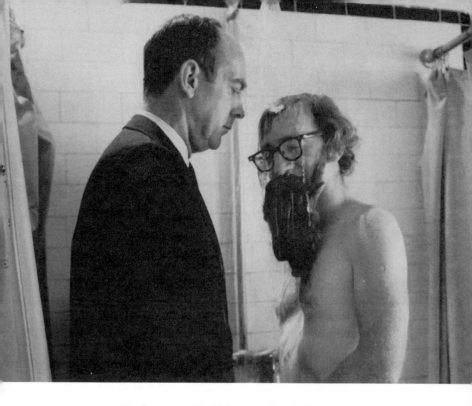

*Woody gets caught with his pants down in "Bananas."*

Allen announces his standard "movie within a movie" technique when, as Starkwell, he hires an out–of–work director to pretend he's filming Allen's gang's bank heist for a movie. Alas, a rival gang shows up at the same bank with the same idea. Includes classic jail sequences and a hilarious interview with Starkwell's parents. Allen's later effort, *Bananas*, also demonstrates the unpolished, frantic, early Allen style. Here, Allen plays an angst–ridden product tester from New York, Fielding Mellish. In his clumsy efforts to woo Lasser, a devout political activist, Allen ends up in San Marcos masquerading as the president of the shaky Latin–American dictatorship. Non–stop shtick is intermittently right on target and missing by a mile. Catch cameos by Sly Stallone and Allen Garfield. Witty score is compliments of the very friendly Marvin Hamlisch.

# Young Doctors in Love

**(1982) 95m R**

Michael McKean, Sean Young, Dabney Coleman, Hector Elizondo,
Patrick Macnee, Pamela Reed;
**Cameos:** Demi Moore, Garry Marshall, Janine Turner
**D:** Gary Marshall
**P:** Jerry Bruckheimer, Gary Marshall
**C:** Donald Peterman
**S:** Michael Elias, Rich Eustis
**M:** Maurice Jarre

Inspired by the broad satire of disaster flicks in *Airplane!*, Marshall produced and directed this memorable spoof of hospital soaps. *Young Doctors in Love* follows the first year of residency for a group of interns at City Hospital. As the seasons change, so do the crazy antics among the medical staff. Interns include McKean as Simon McCormick, an egotistical student vowing to become the world's greatest surgeon, if only he can stop freaking out at the sight of blood, and Young as Stephanie Brody, who is inflicted with a strangely pronounced chronic illness. They add to the insanity, but still find time to fall in love. Heavy dosage of buffoonery is executed by a hilarious supporting cast, including Stanton as drunken pathologist Dr. Carl Ludwig, who has tasted every fluid of the human body, and Richards (*Seinfeld*'s Kramer) as a clumsy hit man from Jersey who gets mistaken for a patient with agonizing results. Along for the ride are stars from *All My Children* and *General Hospital*. After a visit to this hospital, you may not drink apple juice for a while.

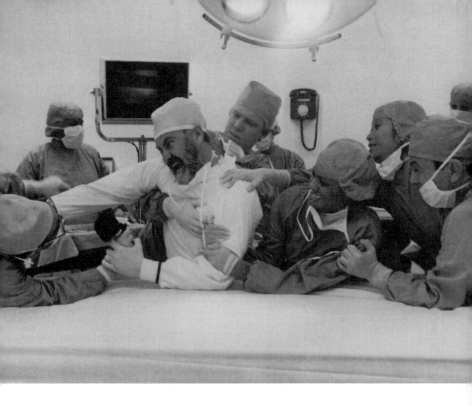

*An early pilot of "ER"*

---

**Attention E.T.: Phone home.**

*Heard over the PA system at the hospital*

---

# Home Alone

**(1990) 105m PG**
Macaulay Culkin, Catherine O'Hara, Joe Pesci, Daniel Stern, John Heard,
Roberts Blossom, John Candy, Billie Bird, Angela Goethals, Devin Ratray,
Kieran Culkin
**D:** Chris Columbus
**P:** John Hughes
**C:** Julio Macat
**S:** John Hughes
**M:** John Williams

The sixth highest grossing film of all time...it's bigger than *Jaws*,
it's bigger than *Batman*, it's bigger than *Roseanne*, and it's a stu-
pidfest to boot, proving that when it comes to creating box office
magic with lowbrow slapstick delirium and sadistic humor, producer Hughes and director Columbus occupy the upper strata of
American filmmaking. Our story begins when belittled and
diminutive Kevin (Culkin) is accidentally left behind when his
family (numbering about 35 by our count) leaves for a Christmas
vacation in France. By the time his parents realize that more
than a few pieces of luggage are missing, they're halfway across
the Atlantic. Meanwhile, Kevin is enjoying the absence of
parental guidance and obnoxious siblings. But the fun is short-
lived as a pair of bumbling robbers (Pesci and Stern, creating a
classic comic duo) plan to raid the house of all its goodies on
X–mas. Kevin, realizing his danger, boobytraps the home with
contraptions that could put MacGyver to shame. He swings
paint cans from banisters, creates mini landmines with Christmas ornaments, and uses a hot iron as a ballistic missile. The
criminals are exposed to Kevin's arsenal with painfully cartoonish outcomes, which, on the guffaw meter, register an 8.5. Brutal, yes, but hilarious. Unless you're Jason Voorhees, you'll never
survive this kid's wrath. Stern and Pesci should have won Oscars
for "Best Stunned Appearances in Supporting Roles." Meanwhile, mother O'Hara desperately tries to get back home, eventually spending time in a van with a polka band headed by Candy.
Overall, a suspicious mixture of humor, violence, and heart-

*Culkin in a familiar pose.*

warming sentimentality (did we mention the scary old guy that Kevin reunites with his family?). *Home Alone 2: Lost in New York* mines the same story vein in a new location. Once again, the family departs for holiday vacation (to Florida) while Kevin is lost in the excitement and lands instead at the Big Apple's Plaza Hotel, where suspicious hotel manager Tim Curry is the least of his problems. Coincidence finds Pesci and Stern, freshly sprung from prison, also visiting the city, where they of course spot Kevin. Fresh from *My Left Foot* and determined to get that art film thing out of her system, Brenda Fricker wanders about as a mystical bag woman supported by an entourage of pigeons. She befriends our little hero as he once again devises ingenious methods for torturing the bad buys, who refuse to learn from their prior cinematic experience. Personally, we'd give the kid a wide berth and go about our business. You'll laugh, you'll cry, you'll wonder why.

# Pauly Shore
# Film Festival
## Son-In-Law

**(1993) 95m PG-13**
Pauly Shore, Carla Gugino, Lane Smith, Cindy Pickett, Mason Adams,
Patrick Renna, Dennis Burkley, Dan Gauthier
**D:** Steve Rash **P:** Peter M. Lenkov, Michael Rotenberg
**C:** Peter Deming **S:** Fax Bahr, Patrick J. Clifton, Peter M. Lenkov, Susan
Martin, Shawn Schepps, Adam Small **M:** Richard Gibbs

## Encino Man

**(1992) 88m PG**
Sean Astin, Brendan Fraser, Pauly Shore, Megan Ward, Robin Tunney, Rick
Ducommon, Mariette Hartley, Richard Masur, Michael DeLuise
**D:** Les Mayfield **P:** George Zaloom **C:** Robert Brinkmann
**S:** Shawn Schepps, George Zaloom **M:** Jonathan Sheffer

A list of dumb movies without a Pauly Shore flick is like a Stallone movie without gratuitous dead. Shore's MTV shtick hits the big screen when the too cool surfer dude goes to college and falls for a naive country gal. He works his magic and transforms her into his own little surfer bimbo, and she sees him as the answer to her prayers-or at least as a false fiancee to throw the farmer boy at home off the trail. She takes him to the family farm for Thanksgiving and Pauly unleashes his alter ego, "The Wease," on the unsuspecting family (you almost feel sorry for them). Much of the humor comes from watching Pauly flounder in the foreign environment known as rural U.S.A. A plot like this one should automatically qualify *Son-In-Law* for a list of dumb movies, but Pauly does have his funny moments that make it a sure thing. If you're not already sick of hearing "hey buddy, it's the Weasel!" in that neo-valley talk of Shore's, you might actually find this entertaining. Better by a bone (or at least fresher) is the Cro-Magnon comedy, *Encino Man* (or as they know it in Olde Englande, *California Man*). While digging their own swimming pool to host an

*Pauley Shore gets Jurassic as Stoney.*

after–prom bash (in a rather drastic attempt to make friends), two semi–spastic seniors at Encino High unearth (and then de–ice) a 10,000 year–old caveman (Fraser), whom they nickname "Link" (as in missing). After giving him a makeover (complete with appropriate hair and bitchin' duds) and teaching him the bare necessities of life, like the four basic food groups (Milk Duds in the dairy group, Sweet Tarts in the fruit group), they use the gnarly cavedude as their ticket to popularity and dates to the prom. One–joke premise is cleverly brought in at under 90 minutes.

# History of the World: Part 1

**(1981) 90m R**

Mel Brooks, Dom DeLuise, Madeline Kahn, Gregory Hines, Harvey Korman,
Cloris Leachman, Pamela Stephenson, Sid Ceasar, Ron Carey, Shecky
Greene, Jackie Mason, Bea Arthur, Henny Youngman

**D:** Mel Brooks
**P:** Mel Brooks
**C:** Woody Omens
**S:** Mel Brooks
**M:** John Morris

The Dawn of Man, Roman Empire, Spanish Inquisition, and French Revolution provide the backdrops as Brooks parodies historical epics like *Ben–Hur* and *The Ten Commandments* using an episodic storyline, old gags, and even older comedians in numerous cameos. Orson Welles' narration brings the proper air of pomposity to the proceedings. Brooks, saving himself bundles in casting, plays many of the main characters, most notably Comicus, the stand–up philosopher in Rome and the challenging dual role of King Louis XVI/royal piss boy. His big musical number during the Spanish Inquisition, while maybe not in the best of taste, at least features swimming nuns and Jackie Mason singing. The humor, in typical Brooks fashion, is hit or miss, with plenty of bits on sex, drugs, and religion mixed with the reliably quotable ("It's good to be the king") Brooksian dialogue. Silly and fast–paced lesser Brooks has enough moments to make it a genuine laugh fest. We're still waiting for Part 2.

> **O**h, Bob. Do I have any openings
> that this man might fit?
>
> *Empress Nympho asks about employment*
> *opportunities for Josephus*

*Mel and friends escaping the wrath of Emperor Nero.*

# Where's Poppa?

**(1970) 84mC R**
George Segal, Ruth Gordon, Ron Liebman, Vincent Gardenia,
Rob Reiner, Trish Van Devere
**D:** Carl Reiner
**P:** Jerry Tokofsky
**C:** Jack Priestley
**S:** Robert Klane, based on his novel
**M:** Jack Elliot

Director Reiner's offbeat Oedipal gem assaults previous norms of
the Golden Age of cinema while telling the story of one Jewish
lawyer's big problem. Gordon (Segal) isn't living a nightmare; his
problem is that his nightmare is still living. Gordon's senile, bor-
derline psychotic mother (Ruth Gordon) makes it impossible for
Gordon to have a girlfriend. She lives to reverently gaze at the
television, ingest a tantalizing culinary combination of Pepsi and
Lucky Charms, and to severely nag and embarrass her poor son.
Over and over she asks, "Where's poppa?" in reference to her dead
husband, whom she no longer remembers is dead. Driven to dis-
traction and then to murder, Gordon plots to kill mom, who
though insane, is one tough old bird madly in love with Gordie.
Or at least very possessive. She reveals her twisted love in an
unforgettable scene in which she kisses Gordon's bare behind in
front of a potential girlfriend, resulting in the woman quickly
exiting out of the apartment. Other outlandish and tasteless gags
involve muggings, rape, nursing homes, and Vietnam War brutal-
ities, lending the picture a delicate sense of vulgar black comedy
that is still revered on college campuses today. Re-released once
as *Going Ape*, apparently just to confuse people.

*George Segal dons a gorilla suit and goes ape over his momma.*

**If you mess this up for me, I'll punch your heart out!**

*George Segal warns his extremely annoying mother when he invites his new girlfriend over*

# Kentucky Fried Movie

**(1977) 78m**

Bill Bixby, Donald Sutherland, Henry Gibson, George Lazenby, Evan Kim,
Master Bong Soo Han, Tony Dow, Boni Enten

**D:** John Landis
**P:** Robert K. Weiss
**C:** Stephen M. Katz
**S:** Jim Abrahams, David Zucker, Jerry Zucker

One of the most successful independent movies ever made launched the comedy career of Landis, who directed *Animal House* next, and was the freshman script from the Zucker Abrahams Zucker team, who used their new clout to fly *Airplane!*. It's a technically proficient, often tasteless sketch comedy that lampoons TV commercials, movies, and contemporary society. A kung-fu parody that pits two actual martial arts experts together in an extremely lavish environment is the funniest segment. The lengthy Bruce Lee takeoff is a black and white spoof of the old courtroom TV shows, while Pam Grier action fests are mocked in "Cleopatra Schwartz," featuring a black Amazon woman married to a rabbi. Sometimes vulgar, often hysterical. The idea originated from skits developed by Kentucky Fried Theater-a Second City wannabe group formed by ZAZ while students at the University of Wisconsin in the early '70s.

---

**Pop quiz: Match the *Fried* cast member to the TV show they appeared in:**

Laugh-In

Leave it to Beaver

My Favorite Martian

Rituals

---

# Medusa: Dare to Be Truthful

**(1992) 54m**
Julie Brown, Bob Goldthwait, Chris Elliott, Stanley DeSantis
**D:** John Fortenberry
**S:** Julie Brown, Charles Coffey
**P:** Ken Walz

Performing a canny spoof (originally for cable TV) of the Material Girl's now famous tour rockumentary, *Truth or Dare*, Brown delivers a celebrity–shredding bull's–eye in this silly send–up of chameleon–like self–promoter Madonna. We follow pop star Medusa (Brown) through fits of egotism and temper tantrums on "The Blonde Leading the Blonde" world tour. From her annoying lollipop sucking during the pre–gig prayer sessions ("God, please give my dancers the wisdom not to f**k up") to her "maternal" feeling toward her dancers ("they're like my children") Brown has the pop diva bit down to a science and no intimate detail of the Material Girl's not–so–personal life escapes unscathed. Medusa is surrounded by eager–to–please flunkies, including Elliot as a pretentious choreographer and DeSantis as manager Benny, who shamelessly strokes her bruised ego after events like a disastrous performance in the Philippines under a shower of volcanic ash or after being accidentally electrocuted in one number. (Medusa: "Are you saying I do my best work when I'm being electrocuted?" Benny: " You were great! They loved it! It was the best part of the show!" Medusa: "O.K. we'll keep it in—but with a lot less voltage.") Medusa also has a string of suspiciously familiar sounding cohorts, and in one scene, phones her famous actor boyfriend Wallace Blatty to inform him that tour is no longer in the Philippines, but in Manilla. Medusa, eager to show her serious side, takes acting lessons from her ex–husband, "psycho" actor Shane Pencil, in order to play Juliet. He explains to her that Juliet would not be grabbing her crotch and trying to be sexy, but instead is devastated that Romeo is dead. Medusa can't quite grasp the concept: "If he's dead, then I have to be extra sexy to get a new boyfriend—you can't doodle with a dead noodle, ha ha!" Brown even recreates the famous scene from Ms. M's movie when she insults the ever–wholesome Kevin Costner, substituting Bobcat Goldthwait as the offended party. The highlights of this Madonna smear–fest, however, are the riotous, wonderfully written (Brown co–wrote this gem) and performed song and dance numbers. A somber, pious Medusa begins one number dressed in priestly robes and holding a rosary, which she later playfully doffs to reveal a bustier and crooning, "C'mon you know, you're invited, to the party in my pants" before moving into the equally hilarious "Vague." But if that isn't enough to have you in stitches, there's a scene that will have even Madonna aficionados laughing out loud, as she, artfully using fruit in a not–so–subtle manner, shows viewers how she became a star.

### You're so fired!

*Medusa, often, to her employees*

# All You Need Is Cash

**(1978) 70m**
Eric Idle, Neil Innes, Rikki Fataar, Dan Aykroyd, Gilda Radner, John Belushi,
George Harrison, Gary Weiss
**D:** Eric Idle, Gary Weis
**P:** Craig Kellem, Gary Weis
**C:** Gary Weis
**S:** Eric Idle
**M:** Neil Innes

Mock rockumentary (also known as *The Rutles*), originally shown in the U.S. on NBC–TV, traces the history of the "Pre–Fab" Four, The Rutles—Dirk, Stig, Nasty, and Barry—from their first single, "Twist and Rut" in 1962, to their films, *A Hard Day's Rut* (1964), *Ouch!* (1965), and *Tragical History Tour* (1968), to their final film and album, *Let It Rot* (1969). Hilarious and shameless Beatles parody is a Monty Python/*Saturday Night Live* hybrid written and directed by Pythoner Eric Idle and *SNL*'s Gary Weis (Lorne Michaels was executive producer). Idle also stars in multiple roles, including the Rutles' McCartney–like bass player Dirk McQuickly, and the Rutles' interviewer, who, in classic Pythonesque fashion, experiences journalistic difficulties in each narration sequence, as he runs down the street after the car–mounted camera and collides with it, trips, bumps into

---

### The Rutles at a press conference after meeting the Queen:

**Reporter:** It must have been a great honor meeting the Queen.

**Nasty:** Yeah. It must've been.

**Reporter:** Do you feel better after seeing the Queen?

**Nasty:** No, you feel better after seeing the doctor.

**Dirk:** Not my doctor, you don't.

obstacles, wades through knee–deep water, and experiences several power outtages. Features a plethora of biggies: George Harrison as a reporter; Mick Jagger as himself and his then–wife, Bianca, as Dirk's wife, Martini; Michael Palin as the Rutles' press agent; *SNL* alumni Dan Aykroyd as "the man who turned down the Rutles;" John Belushi as Ron DeCline, "the most feared promoter in the world;" Bill Murray as "Murray the K;" Gilda Radner and Paul Simon; and the Stones' Ron Wood as a Hell's Angel. Music and lyrics by Neil Innes, who plays the Lennon–like Ron Nasty. (The George Harrison–modeled Stig O'Hara is interestingly played by an Asian actor, Rikki Fataar.) Besides taking on the Holy Grail of Rock and Roll, the mockumentary is distinct from several others on the *Idiot's* list because it was not inspired by but was the inspiration for *This Is Spinal Tap*, a dubious honor, but one that must be acknowledged. The deaths of Lennon, Belushi, and Radner since its release add to the legend. Plus, it's hard to find in our local video stores. Buy the soundtrack and play it backward for a surprise, but don't let your mom catch you.

# Rock 'n' Roll
# High School

**(1979) 94m PG**
The Ramones, P.J. Soles, Vincent Van Patten, Clint Howard, Dey Young,
Mary Woronov, Alix Elias, Dick Miller, Paul Bartel
**D:** Allan Arkush
**P:** Michael Finnell
**C:** Dean Cundey
**S:** Joe Dante, Russ Dvonch, Joseph McBride, Richard Whitley
**M:** The Ramones

Well, if it ain't another of those darn teenage cult movies (and another written by escapees from *The National Lampoon*). Hey, kids! Wanna whole lotta laughs? They don't know much about history, they don't know much biology, but they do know how to rock 'n' roll at lowbrow Vince Lombardi High School nee Rock 'n' Roll High School! The Ramones are the driving force and beat behind cheerleader Riff Randell's (Soles) decision to skip school to buy tickets for their concert, thus securing the wrath of principal Togar (Woronov), who seeks an end to rock music in her school. And with good reason: the last three principals suffered on–the–job nervous breakdowns caused by the unruly student body. The romantic angle in this nonsensical teenfest is supplied by Van Patten, playing dorky football player Tom Roberts. He lusts after Riff, and consults with bathroom guru Eaglebauer (Clint Howard, here without benefit of his brother Ron's direction). Meanwhile, Togar and her goons take their anti–rock rampage too far, confiscating Riff's concert tickets and generally alienating the younger generation who, after an attempted record burning, join forces to put the backbeat back in school before demolishing it. Roamin' the halls with the Ramones isn't a bad way to get an education. Instantly recognizable songs include "Teenage Lobotomy," "Blitzkrieg Bop," "I Wanna Be Sedated," and the title track. Followed less successfully over a decade later by the Corey Feldman exercise in futility, *Rock 'n' Roll High School Forever*.

# Buffy, the Vampire Slayer

**(1992) 98m PG–13**
Kristy Swanson, Donald Sutherland, Luke Perry, Paul "Pee Wee Herman"
Reubens, Rutger Hauer, Michele Abrams, Hilary Swank
**D:** Fran Rubel Kazui
**P:** Kaz Kuzui, Howard Rosenman
**C:** James Hayman
**S:** Joss Whedon
**M:** Carter Burwell

*Beverly Hills 90210* + *Valley Girl* + *Dracula* – Renfield and Shannen Doherty = *Buffy*. Popular cheerleader Buffy (Swanson) seems like your average teenager with suburban dreams ("All I want to do is graduate high school, go to Europe, marry Christian Slater, and die"), until mysterious stranger Merrick (Sutherland) creeps into her "lite" southern California world, which lately has seemed more like the Twilight Zone. Something strange is afoot at the L.A. malls, and the TV news reports a rise in deaths with a unique signature. As one newscasters reports "...the deceased had a mark that was described by one bystander as resembling 'a really gross hickey.'" Merrick thus informs Buffy of the true nature of the menace to her community and of her vampire slaying legacy. Understandably skeptical, she eventually warms to the idea and, after some good hard vampire defense training, starts offing the bloodsuckers with flair, style, and darn good fashion sense. The characters are timely spoofs of themselves, like the high school basketball coach whose new age style motivation includes chastising one of his players, now a vampire. "You missed practice yesterday, Mister. Now I want you to sit down and think about how that made me feel," and to his team, "Remember, I am a person, I have a right to the ball." Buffy's popular cheerleader friends are typical airheaded mall queens whose extremely up–to–date knowledge of in–style clothing forces one to inform Buffy that her choice of jackets is "sooo five minutes ago." Weenie–in–distress Perry supplies an unlikely romantic interest and a bad haircut. Reubens (you know him as Pee Wee Herman) steps out of

*Paul Reubens shows Luke Perry who's boss.*

character and into perhaps the longest death scene yet filmed as the vampire king's right–hand man. Blink and you'll miss Gen–X'er talk show princess and former John Waters muse Ricki Lake as a waitress. Spoofing teen movies, the vampire legend, valley girls, and touchy–feely new age teaching, *Buffy* drives a stake through every cliché it encounters.

# 1941

**(1979) 120m PG**

John Belushi, Dan Aykroyd, Patti LuPone, Ned Beatty, Murray Hamilton,
Treat Williams, Toshiro Mifune, Slim Pickens, Christopher Lee,
Tim Matheson, Robert Stack, Nancy Allen, Warren Oates, Elisha Cook Jr.,
Lorraine Gary, Mickey Rourke, John Candy
**D:** Steven Spielberg
**P:** Buzz Feitshans
**C:** William A. Fraker
**S:** Robert Zemeckis, Bob Gale, John Milius
**M:** John Williams

Critically panned when released, this war drama parody has
achieved a certain air of comedic majesty in the intervening
years. Or at least a reputation for elaborate set pyrotechnics done
in true Little Stevie "this will make 'em drop their popcorn"
fashion. When in doubt, blow something up. Spielberg's
big–budget ($35 million plus, a lot of money in those days),
big–effect, extremely loud and looney version of *The Russians
Are Coming, The Russians Are Coming!* is a chaotic stew of slapstick and big intentions which has its guffaw moments amid the
ruins. Proving that the term "civil defense" is as much an oxy-
moron as "military intelligence," *1941* attempts to capture in
extremely broad comedic strokes the paranoia and chaos that
ruled the California coast after Pearl Harbor. The plot serves
basically to string together big set pieces built around an antici-
pated Japanese attack on the mainland. Belushi does Bluto Blu-
tarsky with a pilot's license, basically reprising his *Animal House*
role in period avaitor drag. Aykroyd, in his first major film, is
amusing as a disoriented tank commander. ("I'm a bug! I'm a
bug! Bzzzzz! Ah ha ha ha!") Beatty steals every scene he's in as
an overly protective homeowner with access to some heavy
artillery. More than half the fun is watching Spielberg work the
special effects lab and choreograph the very expensive slapstick.

*John Belushi comes in for a landing.*

## Belushi & Aykroyd Celluloid

All You Need Is Cash (1978)          Neighbors (1981)

Blues Brothers (1980)

# Tapeheads

**(1989) 93m R**
John Cusack, Tim Robbins, Mary Crosby, Connie Stevens,
Susan Tyrell, Lyle Alzado, Doug McClure
**D:** Bill Fishman
**P:** Peter McCarthy, Michael Nesmith
**C:** Bojan Bazelli
**S:** Bill Fishman, James Herzfeld, Peter McCarthy, Ryan Rowe
**M:** Fishbone, David Kahne

The object of a small cult whose members are unknown to each other, *Tapeheads* boasts a motoring comic duo in Cusack and Robbins. This offbeat, hyperactive comedy is another biting satire on the music industry, and it's sometimes difficult to spoof a business that's already a parody. Security guards Cusack and Robbins want to break into the rock video business. Robbins is the video genius, Cusack the fast–talking, hard–selling business-man. After a series of fairly funny money–making ventures, they make it big, but find themselves on the run from the Secret Service due to a certain incriminating video faux pas. Robbins later sang his way into big time politics via *Bob Roberts*, proving he can play both sides of the aisle. Lookout for a host of music biz cameos, as Stiv Bators, Sam Moore, Junior Walker, Martha Quinn, Ted Nugent, and Weird Al Yankovic walk on.

---

## We love the Swanky Modes!

*Josh and Ivan, in unison,
state their musical preference*

---

*John Cusack and Tim Robbins discuss the best way to pass a sobriety test.*

Sorry, guys. The Brothers Against Drunk Driving, they've been busting my ass. You've gotta perform a sobriety test. (...) Close your eyes. Real tight. No peeking. Now, recite the alphabet backward, skipping all the vowels, and give me the sign language for each letter as you pass by.

# The Party

**(1968) 99m**
Peter Sellers, Claudine Longet, Marge Champion, Sharron Kimberly,
Denny Miller, Gavin MacLeod
**D:** Blake Edwards
**P:** Blake Edwards
**C:** Lucien Ballard
**S:** Blake Edwards, Frank Waldman, Tom Waldman
**M:** Henry Mancini

*Gandhi* meets *The Pink Panther* in this hilarious '60s spoof. Imported to Hollywood from his native India to make *The Son of Gunga Din*, Sellers is a language–addled disaster catalyst who proceeds to accidentally destroy everything in sight. After he manages to level the film's crucial set, the producer wants him deported, but instead Sellers is erroneously invited to a party at the producer's house. Once there, he bumbles innocently through the mansion, wreaking more havoc than a herd of elephants, and more importantly, one baby elephant. Two incidents, the billiards game and the washing of the clothes, illustrate the moral of the story: when a slightly confused and definitely clumsy strange little man offers his assistance, you should decline. Edwards, who also had directed Sellers in 1964's bumbling detective fests *The Pink Panther* and *A Shot in the Dark*, proves once again that he's the master of one–joke gagfests, while Sellers further refines his soon–to–be–classic Clouseauness. *The Party*, like just about anything with Sellers, bears repeated viewings to catch the smaller, subtle gags inside the broad physical humor.

*Peter Sellers displays a rare moment of grace.*

# License to Drive

**(1988) 88m PG–13**
Corey Haim, Corey Feldman, Carol Kane, Richard Masur, Nina Siemaszko,
Heather Graham, Michael Manasseri, Harvey Miller, M. A. Nickles,
Helen Hanft, James Avery
**D:** Greg Beeman
**P:** Andrew Licht, Jeffrey A. Mueller
**C:** Bruce Surtees
**S:** Neil Tolkin
**M:** Jay Ferguson

"Dude, you can do anything, you have a license." Before there
was Bill and Ted and Beavis and Butthead, Corey and Corey ruled
the airwaves. The former adolescent dream duo and *Teen Beat*
coverboys were the top idols of the pubescent set in the '80s, but
it was a much more innocent time, not yet witness to cata-
clysmic events like Whitewater and the Disney/Cap City merger.
Before personal problems, parental disparities, drugs, and the
aging process took their toll, The Coreys saw their stardom peak
with this whimsical teen romp about how a driver's license-or
lack thereof—can affect the life of a horny teenaged boy and his
party–hardy pals.  For 16–year–old Les (Corey H.), flunking his
driving exam means suffering all the typical indignities of not
having a driver's license, like being forced to ride the school bus
and having his dad dropping him off for dates, and like watching
sports car studs get all the chicks. Life can be so bogue. But rag-
ing hormones and an antagonistic buddy named Dean (Corey F.)
will not allow Les to miss the opportunity of a lifetime. When he
gets a hot date with a major babe (Graham), he scams his grandpa's primo Caddy for a night on the town that turns into a
one–car demolition derby. As Les says, "An innocent girl, a
harmless drive, what could possibly go wrong?" Car parts collide,
car parts fall off, car parts get barfed on, and everybody takes
turns looking at each other and shouting "Oh, shit!" right before
the remaining car parts become airborne. Feldman later admit-
ted to being coked up for much of the shoot, which only adds to
the adolescent charm of this period piece.

*Teen dreams hit the mean streets.*

| Corey Mania | |
|---|---|
| Dream a Little Dream 2 (1994) | Dream a Little Dream (1989) |
| National Lampoon's Last Resort (1994) | The Lost Boys (1987) |
| Blown Away (1993) | |

# Tommy Boy

**(1995) 96m PG–13**
Chris Farley, David Spade, Rob Lowe, Bo Derek, Brian Dennehy,
Julie Warner, Sean McCann
**D:** Peter Segal
**P:** Lorne Michaels
**C:** Victor J. Kemper
**S:** Bonnie Turner, Terry Turner
**M:** Michael Muhlfriedel, David Newman, Steven Soles

Yes, another classic comedy team has arrived, one a big fat guy and the other a skinny little snob as Gen–X meets Laurel and Hardy. In his first starring role, Farley belly flops onto the big screen as the lovable, obese simpleton, Tommy Callahan. And he's a simpleton for the ages, having spent seven years in college, only to graduate with a D+ average. But he gets straight A's as a comic misfit, waddling clumsily, bumping into doors and walls with his practiced *SNL* slapstick. Tommy must save his late dad's (Dennehy, who better?) auto parts empire from his conniv-

---

### More Important Facts About *Tommy*

Based on *The Who*'s groundbreaking rock opera.

Spade and Farley first appeared together in *Coneheads*.

Spade and Farley will appear together again in *Black Sheep*. Spade plays a political candidate and Farley flexes those acting muscles as his oafish, embarrassing brother.

Even though the movie is set in Sandusky, Ohio, it was cleverly filmed on location in Toronto, Canada, to save money on the big ice hockey scene.

Screenwriters Bonnie and Terry Turner wrote *The Brady Bunch Movie*, *Wayne's World I & II*, and *Coneheads*. So don't mess with them.

Dan Aykroyd has an uncredited cameo as a slimy mogul.

---

*Tommy is excited as he gets his first job in the family business.*

ing stepmother (Derek, in a rare non–swimsuit appearance) and step–brother (Lowe, not stretching far from his role in *Wayne's World*). In order to prevent the sale of the auto parts business and the loss of thousands of jobs in his home town of Sandusky, Ohio, Tommy and number–crunching, know–it–all accountant Richard (Spade) hit the road to drum up more business. They discover they have many personal differences, fueled by Tommy's unpredictable gastronomic disturbances and Richard's deadpan sarcasm. (Tommy: "Lot's of people spend seven years in college." Richard: "Yeah, they're called doctors.") The rocky road is blessed with lots of gags in bad taste and one of film's more amusing encounters with a deer. A small theatrical package achieving sizable stupidity, goofiness and charm.

# Putney Swope

**(1969) 85m R**
Arnold Johnson, Antonio Fargas, Allen Garfield, Stanley Gottlieb,
Archie Russell, Ramone Gordon, Bert Lawrence, Joe Engler, Allan Arbus
**D:** Robert Downey Sr.
**P:** Robert Downey Sr.
**C:** Gerald Cotts
**S:** Robert Downey Sr.
**M:** Charles Cuva

Broad swipe at the advertising industry and racial stereotypes was made on a shoestring and looks like it was shot with a camcorder, but its underground pedigree has earned *Swope* the title of "cult classic." Of course, most of the cult has since passed on, engaging in stockbrokering and other more appropriate mid–life pursuits, but *Swope* has a way of rearing its funky little head every few years and is enjoying a mini–renaissance now, since we went out and bought the movie. The usual stiff, all–white ad agency is taken over by black radicals after the board of directors accidentally elects Putney (Johnson), the token black member, as chairman. Soon the agency is turning out hit but irreverent spots on pimple creams, cereal, and mousetraps and basking in the gratitude of its goofy white clients. Even U.S. President Mimeo, convincingly played by a midget (Pepi Hermine), asks for Putney's help. Fame and fortune cause problems, however. It's not exactly a finely tuned script, the acting sort of sucks, the score is goofy '60s elevator music, and a lot of the satire seems dated, making you wonder what all the fuss was about when it was first not released. But it's generally silly and kind of fascinating as a socio–cultural time capsule. Director/writer Downey, father of junior the actor, next delighted the non–masses with *Greaser's Palace*, a satiric Christ allegory.

# Fatal Instinct

**(1993) 89m PG–13**
Armand Assante, Sherilyn Fenn, Kate Nelligan, Sean Young,
Christopher McDonald, James Remar, Tony Randall,
Clarence Clemmons, Michael Cumpsy
**D:** Carl Reiner

Take the most memorable parts of *Fatal Attraction, Basic Instinct, Double Indemnity, 9 1/2 Weeks, Sleeping with the Enemy, Body Heat, Cape Fear,* and *The Postman Always Rings Twice,* add the standard noir cliches, and mix it all up with equal parts mockery and gall. Viola! *Fatal Instinct* emerges, a wacky spoof bent on telling an entire genre to lighten up. Promising more than it delivers, it still supplies enough low-rent laughs to make it an arresting moment in spoof history. Assante is Ned Ravine, a dim detective/lawyer (he arrests 'em, then defends 'em). His loyal girl Friday Laura (Fenn) keeps his life in order, while fending off tormented flashbacks of her husband's obsession with straight bathroom towels. Ravine's cheating wife Lana (Nelligan) and her grease monkey lover Frank (McDonald) hatch a crazy plot to murder Ned based on a triple indemnity clause in his life insurance (he has to die after being shot on a northbound train and falling into a river before she can collect). Ned also gets mixed up with Lola (Young), a femme fatale with a big secret who'd be particularly fetching if she didn't always have something stuck to the bottom of her shoe (gum, candy wrappers, toilet paper, car mats, etc.). He's also being stalked by tattooed (with Pee Wee Herman and Bart Simpson quotes, nonetheless) ex–client Max Shady (Remar) who blames Ned for sending him up the river. The nonsensical plot unmercifully spoofs everything sacred noir, including the moody sax background played by a very-much on–camera Clarence Clemmons. Much of the fun lies in recognizing Reiner's gag targets (among the more obscure: Ned is called "mambo king;" Lola falls to her death via a broken stair rail, ala Young's exit from *No Way Out*), so we recommend a steady grip on the pause and reverse buttons. Ever the auteur, Reiner contributes a Hitchcockian cameo while standing at a urinal.

# The Groove Tube

**(1972) 75m R**
Lane Sarasohn, Chevy Chase, Richard Belzer,
Marcy Mendham, Bill Kemmill
**D:** Ken Shapiro
**P:** Levitt Pickman
**C:** Bob Bailin
**S:** Ken Shapiro, Lane Sarasohn

The context: a television series called *The Groove Tube* that rudely spoofs everything on television from commercials to newscasts. One of the truly innovative comedies to come out of the '70s set the standard for bawdy adolescent comedy with an edge. Writer, director and star Shapiro pokes fun at every aspect of the boob tube. Separate vignettes take potshots at children's shows, cooking programs, talk shows, commercials, and the evening news. Occasionally the humor walks a thin line between pornography and societal commentary, which as thin lines go, proves to be a funny one. One skit involves Koko the clown reading excerpts from Fanny Hill (I had hoped he "might gain swift entrance" and look forward to his "delicious velvet tip") to all the boys and girls. Another skit has a sports program that turns the spotlight on one of the most exciting spectator sports, sex. As commentators watch the West German team in action, they make such observations as there's a "sweep, curve and probe," "thrust, double thrust, true championship action." Then there's the less offensive talk show where the topic is inflation in the free economy, but the panel gets carried away with the tea and donuts. *Tube* provides juvenile perspective on historical events such as Watergate with montage shots of the hearings to the Oscar Peterson medley, "Mumbles." *Tube* not only served as a silly parody of television, but also a provided a stumping ground for Belzer and Chase. Belzer displays his versatility in several skits, depicting characters like a marijuana dealer, a black prostitute, a journalist reporting from Vietnam, and the president of the U.S. He's also the voiceover for the running gag commercial for Uranus Corporation, spoofing huge companies that have the

*Groovin' on "Tube."*

"peoples' interest in mind." Chase makes his feature film debut as a supporting player, two years before he became a not–ready–for–prime–time player. Based on an off–Broadway revenue that ran for five years. Originally rated X, but was edited for R rating.

# Fear of a Black Hat

**(1994) 87m R**
Larry B. Scott, Mark Christopher Lawrence, Rusty Cundieff, Kasi Lemmons
**D:** Rusty Cundieff
**P:** Darin Scott
**C:** John Demps, Jr.
**S:** Rusty Cundieff
**M:** Larry Robinson

If you've seen *This Is Spinal Tap,* you won't have a hard time pigeonholing *Fear* as essentially a rap version of the same movie. This mock rapumentary follows N.W.H. (Niggaz With Hats), the most controversial and heavily armed rap group in the world, for an inside look at the lives of hard–partying but not-so-hard-working rappers. With names like Ice Cold, Tasty-Taste, and Tone-Def, you know you're in for a first–rate satire that would do its predecessor proud. Nina Blackburn, the pseudo–interviewer, asks probing questions about why all of the group's white managers get killed (ala *Tap's* drummers) and exactly why they have so many hats. Watch for the scene where Nina asks leader Ice Cold (Cundieff) about how they arrived at their own special definitions of various sorts of women in many of his group's songs. His response, like most of the jokes in the movie, will not appeal to the politically correct. No stereotype is left untouched as this spoof mercilessly and hilariously picks apart today's rap acts. As with *Tap,* the more the musicians try to explain themselves, the less sense they make.

*The gang from "Porky's."*

## Porky's Gets Panned:

**"One of those movies that makes you weep for the state of the contemporary cinema—and, even more, for the gullibility of the public that pays to see it."**

*Margaret Hinxman,* Daily Mail *(well, it ain't no* "Godfather")

# Ernest Goes to Camp

**(1987) 92m PG**
Jim Varney, Victoria Racimo, John Vernon, Iron Eyes Cody, Lyle Alzado,
Gailard Sartain, Daniel Butler, Hakeem Abdul-Samad
**D:** John R. Cherry III
**P:** Stacy Williams
**C:** Harry Mathias, Jim May
**S:** John R. Cherry III
**M:** Shane Keister

To choose just one Ernest movie from the collected work is a tough job, knowwhatImean? Pea-brained pitchman Ernest P. Worrell stars in the first of the sometimes dreadful but always compellingly dumb series of movies capitalizing on the popularity of Varney's commercial character. Ernest wants to be a counselor in this summer camp farce, and instead lands the position of custodial engineer. As luck would have it, one of the counselors is injured and Ernest does indeed get a chance to advise the biggest delinquents of the camp, who waste no time in getting down to the business of harassing their less-than-genius mentor. Enter bad-guy Bronk Stinson (Alzado) who uses Varney as his unwitting flunky to persuade camp owner Old Indian Chief (Cody) to shut down the place and sign away his land rights. Heroic Ernest must prevent this travesty and leads the misguided youths in an all-out battle, complete with flaming arrows and snapping turtles, to save Camp Kikakee. Check your brain at the door and enjoy mild chuckle spasms throughout.

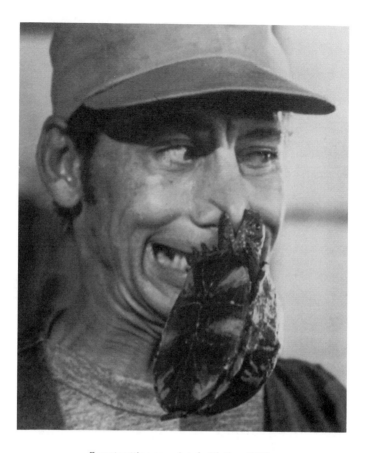

*Ernest getting acquainted with the wildlife.*

**All-Out Ernest**

Slam Dunk Ernest (1995)

Ernest Goes to Jail (1990)

Ernest Rides Again (1993)

Ernest Saves Christmas (1988)

Ernest Scared Stupid(1991)

# Airheads

**1994 PG-13**
Brendan Fraser, Steve Buscemi, Adam Sandler, Chris Farley,
Michael McKean, Judd Nelson, Joe Mantegna, Michael Richards,
Ernie Hudson, Nina Siemaszko, John Melendez, Amy Locane
**D:** Michael Lehmann
**P:** Mark Burg, Robert Simonds
**C:** John Schwartzman
**S:** Rich Wilkes
**M:** Carter Burwell

Anarchy and rock-n-roll are blended into this farce that attempts the heretofore untried compound of *Wayne's World* and *Dog Day Afternoon*. Three members (Fraser, Buscemi, and Sandler) from a basement rock band called the Lone Rangers are determined to get their demo tape heard on the radio. But asking nicely doesn't seem to work, so in their own bumbling manner, they hold up a local radio station, using water pistols to take hostages of the surprised star DJ and stuffy program manager. As the hostage situation is recorded on the air, the event snowballs into a media circus. The Lone Rangers become the darlings of an adoring metalhead crowd short on brains but long on gusto gathering outside the radio station. Somehow, mere plot summary (or for that matter, an autographed copy of the script) will not suffice to explain how the Three Stooges of rock-n-roll become a triumphant underdog symbol for the suppressed youth of America. Borrowing the classic "Attica, Attica" scene from *Dog Day Afternoon,* Fraser riles the crowd by chanting "Rodney King." Occasionally deserted by the writing and directing team, but supported by a cast rich with subversive comedic talents. Mantegna contributes a hip performance as DJ Ian, while McKean is a hoot as the weasely program director. Comes complete with a kickin' soundtrack supplied by White Zombie and The Galactic Cowboys. Don't try to watch this and do your doctoral dissertation at the same time.

*Chazz (Fraser) and Rex (Buscemi) give police their list of demands,
which includes the latest Barry Manilow release.*

## Behind every great script, there's hard-earned experience:

Screenwriter Wilkes actually tried to sneak into Capitol Records before he wrote the scene where Chazz does the same thing—except instead of meeting a top exec, Wilkes was brutalized and thrown out by security.

# Rosencrantz & Guildenstern Are Dead

**(1990) 118m PG**
Gary Oldman, Tim Roth, Richard Dreyfuss, Iain Glen, Joanna Roth,
Joanna Miles, Ian Richardson, Donald Sumpter
**D:** Tom Stoppard
**P:** Emmanuel Azenburg, Michael Brandman
**C:** Peter Biziou
**S:** Tom Stoppard, based on his play
**M:** Brian Gulland, Stanley Myers, Graham Preskett

Heads, you'll like this movie. Tails, you won't (now you'll have to see it just to get this reference). Although playwright Stoppard adapted his absurdist 1967 play for film with less success than he had on the stage, it's still a worthy view. Two confused minor characters of Shakespeare's *Hamlet* squabble rhetorically and completely miss the plot that's tightening fatally around them. Oldman and Roth are hilarious as the dim-witted duo who try to make sense out of their senseless situation. One of their best moments is a verbal tennis match, a gem since neither could be mistaken for a genius. Dreyfuss, as a menacing thespian, tries to hip them to their hopeless circumstances to an amusing conclusion.

---

**Rosencrantz: Is there a choice?**

**Guildenstern: Is there a God?**

**Rosencrantz: Foul! No non sequiturs.**

*R & G explain one rule of*
*their verbal tennis match called "Questions."*

---

*No noose is good noose!*

**Guildenstern:** You're tumblers, then?

**Head Player:** We can give you a tumble, if that is your taste...and times being what they are.

**Rosencrantz:** What exactly is it you do?

**Head Player:** We keep to our usual stuff, more or less, only inside out. We do on stage the things that are supposed to happen off, which is a kind of integrity if you look on every exit as an entrance (slight pause) somewhere else.

*Richard Dreyfuss confuses R & G*

# Police Academy

**(1984) 96m R**
Steve Guttenberg, Kim Cattrall, Bubba Smith, George Gaynes,
Michael Winslow, Leslie Easterbrook, Georgina Spelvin, Debralee Scott
**D:** Hugh Wilson
**P:** Paul Maslansky
**C:** Michael D. Margulies
**S:** Neal Israel, Pat Proft, Hugh Wilson
**M:** Robert Folk

Does for the police department what *Marathon Man* did for dentistry, elevating the stature of *Car 54, Where Are You?* in the process. A big-city police department needs more recruits, so what do they do? Fix it so that just about anyone can be a cop, including normally unemployable actors. Soon the typical band of law-enforcement misfit wannabes are in training to be the city's finest. Guttenberg, as lead flunky who wants to up the academy, has the best bit with his demonstration of proper parking technique. As the dense commandant overlooking it all, Gaynes finds financial security above and beyond *Punky Brewster*. Bailey, as the lead nemesis, plays and encounters a real horse's ass. Broad blue humor and slapstick unsupported by much of a script is probably best appreciated by individuals wanting to get in touch with their inner adolescent. With all the delightful sequels, you'll spend days slapping your head muttering, "I could've written this!"

> **The academy is taking all kinds today.**
> **Anybody can get in. Even you.**
>
> *Captain Reed (Ross)*
> *speaks to Carey Mahoney (Guttenberg).*

*Cmdt. Lassard separates two of his newest recruits, Fackler and Zed, in "Police Academy 3."*

### Freeze! Or They'll Shoot!

Police Academy 2: Their First Assignment (1985)

Police Academy 3: Back in Training (1986)

Police Academy 4: Citizens on Patrol (1987)

Police Academy 5: Assignment Miami Beach (1988)

Police Academy 6: City Under Siege (1989)

# Coneheads

**(1993) 86m PG**
Dan Aykroyd, Jane Curtin, Laraine Newman, Jason Alexander,
Michelle Burke, Chris Farley, Michael Richards, Michael McKeon,
David Spade, Jan Hooks, Julia Sweeney, Lisa Jane Persky
**D:** Steven Barron

Stranded on Earth, Aykroyd and Curtin reprise their roles as Beldar and Prymaat, the elders of the family from France (but really aliens from Remulak) who are just trying to fit in. Stuffed with cast members from *Saturday Night Live* past and present (and maybe future, as Aykroyd's toddler daughter Danielle makes her film debut), the comedy all-stars provide the film with a lift. Newman, who created the role of daughter Connie, appears as Beldar's sister, while Burke takes over as the teen. Farley is the love interest of Connie and finds himself astounded at the furious speed at which she consumes submarine sandwiches on their first date (he thought only his mother could eat a sub like that). The audience even gets a glimpse of Remulak itself when the family is rescued but finds they no longer fit into their native home. Fans of the original *SNL* skit will enjoy reminiscing over the popular '70s comic shtick, even though it would have done better about a decade earlier. Others will enjoy the parade of recent *SNL* regulars. McKean and Spade steal the show as the two immigration officials out to expose the true identity of the secretive family. They even go as far as to disguise themselves as Jehovah's Witnesses. Promoted with the line, "As much pleasure as can be obtained with your lower extremities still garbed."

*Bald is beautiful.*

# Return of the Living Dead

**(1985) 90m R**

Clu Gulager, James Karen, Linnea Quigley, Don Calfa, Jewel Shepard
**D:** Dan O'Bannon
**P:** Tom Fox
**C:** Jules Brenner
**S:** Dan O' Bannon
**M:** Matt Clifford

An often clever and scary combination of sequel–to and spoof–of Romero's classic horror film. Poisonous gas seeps into a small town and has the natural effect of reviving the inhabitants of the local cemetery. The once *dead* dead now join the ranks of the living dead and raise havoc with the living in their pursuit of eating brains, brains, and still more brains. Punctuated by punk music, exaggerated gore, and outright silliness (Karen has a hilarious scene where he aides in the destruction of a zombie in a warehouse), it's hard to believe that director O'Bannon wrote the creepier and more serious *Alien*. But doubt no further and watch as O'Bannon duplicates one of the eerie scenes from that sci–fi classic by having an embalmer question a mutilated zombie lying on his table, asking the somewhat decomposed somnabulist why zombies eat brains. The movie even begins with the tongue–in–cheek disclaimer, "the events depicted are true." A rash of bad acting by teens who play characters named Trash and Suicide places the film in its true perspective, an outrageous spoof on the living dead sub–genre.

> **I love you—I want to eat your brains!**
>
> *Thom Matthews, a walking corpse who can't decide what he really wants from his living girlfriend, Beverly Randolph*

# House Party

**(1990) 100m**
Christopher Reid, Christopher Martin, Martin Lawrence, Tisha Campbell,
Paul Anthony, A.J. Johnson, Full Force, Robin Harris, John Witherspoon
**D:** Reginald Hudlin
**S:** Reginald Hudlin
**P:** Warrington Hudlin
**C:** Peter Deming
**M:** Marcus Miller

Energetic and silly hip–hop romp showcases rap group Kid 'n' Play in a low-budget box-office hit expanded from writer/director Reggie Hudlin's Harvard short. With a typical *Leave It to Beaver* plot, tower-haired Kid wants to go to his friend Play's ultimate house party. But after a fight in the school cafeteria, he's grounded by his frustrated dad (the late Robin Harris). Kid is not one to let an opportunity of meeting cute girls and a chance at rapping on the microphone escape him, so he sneaks out the house past his sleeping father (enjoying a dose of *Dolemite*). Getting to the party becomes complicated as three hoods (Full Force) hound him, while the cops chase them all. Kid temporarily stops off at a more mature benefit d-jayed by a bored George Clinton. Meanwhile, Dad is awake and stalking the neighborhood, cursing his kid Kid for having a head like an "ol' tree stump." At the house party, the action is electric as hips gyrate and hands wave in the air with some great dance sequences and rap numbers. Martin Lawrence displays early comedic promise as the d.j. who badly wants a date, but whose present girlfriend Hallie (as in halitosis) stands in his way. The further adventures of Kid 'n' Play are followed in two lesser sequels, as the writing/producing/directing Hudlins departed for the animated *Bebe's Kids* (written by Robin Harris) and *Boomerang* with Eddie Murphy. In *House Party II*, Kid 'n' Play hold a pajama jammy jam to raise college tuition. And it's more diminishing returns as *House Party III* focuses on Kid's engagement and subsequent bachelor party.

# Saturday the 14th

**(1981) 91m PG**
Richard Benjamin, Paula Prentiss, Severn Darden, Kevin Brando,
Jeffrey Tambor, Kari Michaelson, Nancy Lee Andrews, Rosemary DeCamp
**D:** Howard R. Cohen
**P:** Julie Corman
**S:** Howard R. Cohen, Jeff Begun

A parody not, as the title suggests, of modern slasher films, but
of the kinder, gentler monster movies of yore. This one's about a
family inheriting a haunted mansion. Prentiss and Benjamin,
who are also off-screen husband and wife, play the unfortunate
couple, with Brando as their son. Brando manages to evoke various vampires and assorted monsters who begin to make their
cameo appearances. Soon the family is engulfed in ghouls who
are there seeking the hidden, ancient "Book of Evil." Lots of
good gags and cast keep it entertaining and fun. Followed by
*Saturday the 14th Strikes Back,* a weak sequel which introduces
another family in another haunted mansion but without the benefit of a strong cast to make it work.

---

### Equally Cheesy Monster Spoofs

Hell Comes to Frogtown (1988)    Strange Invaders (1983)

Repossessed (1990)               Teenage Exorcist (1993)

---

*Oh, the life of a monster—Calgon, take me away!*

# Major League

**(1989) 106m R**
Tom Berenger, Charlie Sheen, Corbin Bernsen, Margaret Whitton, James
Gammon, Rene Russo, Wesley Snipes, Charles Cyphers, Dennis Haysbert,
Bob Uecker
**D:** David S. Ward
**P:** Chris Chesser, Irby Smith
**C:** Reynaldo Villalobos
**S:** David S. Ward
**M:** James Newton Howard

Heeere's the pitch. America's favorite pastime may not be recovering well from the recent strike, but baseball movies are always a hit. Throw in some comedy and you've got a home run. Rich-bitch owner of the Cleveland Indians (back when they were perpetual underachievers) has losing (and moving to Florida) in mind when she assembles a team of scrubs—until the guys find out and rally into champions. You've seen this motley crew of clichéd baseball chuckleheads before—the wise but washed-up veteran catcher, the egomaniac superstar, the superstitious voodoo worshipper, the Bible-thumper, and the wild young pitcher with potential—but never with so many laughs. Sheen is especially fun as the ex-con rock and roll hurler ("What league were you in last year?" "California Penal.") whose control problems earn him the tag "Wild Thing" and make him a fan favorite. The boys go from last to first, in improbable fashion. Stretched to extra innings with a sequel, *Major League 2* (1994) including basically the same plot and cast, but Omar Epps pinch-hits for Snipes. New clichés include a catcher who can't throw the ball back to the pitcher and the former "Wild Thing" going corporate.

*Third baseman Bernsen shows pitcher Sheen what a baseball looks like.*

**W**omen! You can't live without em,
and they can't pee standin' up.

*Rube Baker on relationships in "Major League 2."*

# Zorro, the Gay Blade

**(1981) 96m PG**
George Hamilton, Lauren Hutton, Brenda Vaccaro, Ron Leibman,
Donovan Scott, James Booth
**D:** Peter Medak
**P:** Greg Alt, Don Moriarty
**C:** John A. Alonzo
**S:** Hal Dresner
**M:** Ian Fraser

Hamilton follows his first successful spoof, *Love at First Bite*, with this affectionate send–up of the legendary Latin swashbuckler. In a dual role that must have severely stretched his thespian talents, Hamilton is the gallant swordsman Zorro (of '60s television fame) and his Liberace–like gay twin brother. It seems that Don Diego Vega (Hamilton), son of Zorro, is spurred to take up daddy's mask and sword when a cruel tyrant, Alcalde (Leibman in an over-the-top, at the top-of-his-lungs bit), terrorizes local villagers. After Zorro is injured, his long–lost twin brother, Bunny Wigglesworth, suddenly arrives from England and pledges to help. While Zorro has a flair for the dramatic, Bunny has a flair for fashion, changing the basic black costume to more colorful attire. His motto is, "There is no shame in being poor, only in dressing poor." With this flamboyant assistant, the handsome hunk beats the bad guy and gets the gorgeous girl, Hutton. While the gags eventually run dry, Hamilton, with ham firmly on wry, provides an inspired parody of the masked man in black.

*George Hamilton camping it up to the hilt.*

# Brain Donors

**(1992) 79m PG**
John Turturro, Bob Nelson, Mel Smith, Nancy Marchand, Teri Copley,
George De La Pena, Spike Alexander, John Savident
**D:** Dennis Dugan
**P:** Gil Netter, James D. Brubaker
**C:** David M. Walsh
**S:** Pat Proft
**M:** Ira Newborn

With executive producers David and Jerry Zucker lending their names to the producer credits (and presumedly some bucks) and cohort Pat Proft doing the words, *Brain Donors* is *Problem Child* director Dugan's homage to the Marx Brothers and *A Night at the Opera*, with a fair bit of Loony Tunes madness thrown in for good measure. Bursting with silly repartee in the manner of classic Groucho, a nonsensical plot involving a ballet company, and sight gags galore (many of them revolving around the hidden assets of Harpo mimic Nelson's coat of many surprises), it's still surprisingly flat at times. But what the hell, they really try (particularly Turturro in his Groucho turn), and it's only 79 minutes long! As Flakfizer remarks early on, "Nothing like the thrill of spending an evening watching a bunch of anorexics leaping around guys with bulging genitals." What there is of a plot revolves around desire of newly widowed and fabulously rich Lillian Oglethorpe (Marchand) to create a ballet company in memory of her late husband. Though opposed by stuffy lawyer Laslo (Savident), sleazy lawyer Roland T. Flakfizer (Turturro) and his two zany cohorts (Harpo and Chico) are there to help, or at least to make a quick buck. "Lillian, I have a dream," says Flakfizer at the reading of the will. "We'll bring in a whole new breed of ballet goer with innovative giveaways—leotard night, wet tutu competitions—and we'll be the first company to perform ballet for the hard of hearing: we'll have the ballerinas wearing wooden shoes!" The movie even ventures to restage the famous crowded stateroom scene from *A Night at the Opera*, showing at the very least guts if not skill, and in Dugan's case, we're pretty sure it's

*John Turturro points the finger at fellow donor.*

not *great* skill. Fast-paced and broadly surreal, with Turturro continually sputtering lines and lots of bad jokes, it culminates with a *Swan Lake* in which the dying swan receives CPR, a giant duck joins the dancers, dancing duck hunters and a pack of hounds invade, and the duck is shot dead. Annoying claymation credits by Will Vinton accompanied by annoying theme music by Ira Newborn open and close at length, making the movie several minutes shorter than the 79 minutes credited. And yes, the title is a complete mystery; originally it was entitled *Lame Ducks*.

# Caveman

**(1981) 91m PG**

Ringo Starr, Dennis Quaid, Shelley Long, Jack Gilford, John Matuszak,
Barbara Bach, Cork Hubbert, Mark King, Paco Morayta, Evan Kim,
Ed Greenberg, Carl Lumbly, Jack Scalici
**D:** Carl Gottlieb
**P:** David Foster, Lawrence Turman
**C:** Alan Hume
**S:** Rudy DeLuca, Carl Gottlieb
**M:** Lalo Schifrin

*Atouk aloona Lana. Lana aloona Tonda. Tala aloona Atouk.*
With a script of only 15 English words, you'll have to master
cavespeak quickly to appreciate *Caveman,* undoubtedly the
dumbest movie ever set in One Zillion B.C. (October 9th to be
exact). Okay, so it's not exactly a classic, but this stone age spoof
earns nomination for appropriately casting the Funny Beatle as
Atouk, your average prehistoric guy. Atouk's in love with the lus-
cious, well–oiled, fur bikini–clad Lana (Bach), who provides
proof that ancient women inexplicably had access to Nair. But
Lana belongs to the humongous and very hairy Tonda
(Matuszak), and Atouk's attempts to gain her affection (or at
least get some *zug–zug*) get him bounced from the cave. Atouk
meets up with cave buddy Lar (Quaid) and becomes the leader of
an outcast group, including the lovely Tala (Long). Together
they search for *ool* (food), get caught in a nearby Ice Age, fight
off dinosaurs that look like lame Godzilla movie rejects, and
launch an attack on Tonda and his simian crew. If nothing else,
*Caveman* proves that gags with a decidedly scatological bent are
indeed the oldest jokes in the world. No matter—despite lots of
gross–out moments, classic slapstick rules. Ringo and company
even invent (what else?) rock 'n' roll in one of the niftier scenes.
So relax those overworked synapses and enjoy a goofy journey
into the primitive past.

*Starr rescues wife Bach from the clutches of Dennis Quaid.*

## Cavespeak to English Dictionary:

zug-zug = sex

ool = food

oweey = fire

Abana abou attoma = call my agent, we'll do lunch

# Three O'Clock High

**(1987) PG 97m**
Casey Siemaszko, Anne Ryan, Stacey Glick, Jonathan Wise,
Richard Tyson, Jeffrey Tambor, Liza Morrow, John P. Ryan, Philip Baker Hall
**D:** Phil Joanou
**C:** Barry Sonnenfeld
**W:** Richard Christian Matheson, Thomas Szollosi

Appropriating *Risky Business* (complete with ethereal music by Tangerine Dream) and *Ferris Bueller's Day Off, Three O'Clock High* is a worthy entry in the hell high school category. Siemaszko (complete with bratty sister) is the cute, kinda nerdy high school journalist Jerry Mitchell, who wakes up late on the first day of school, foreshadowing the kind of day it's going to be for our plucky protagonist. His first assignment: a scoop on the new kid in school, whose sullied reputation as a homicidal bully and troublemaker precedes him. Buddy Ravell (Tyson) turns out to be just that, and after a not–so–friendly confrontation with the goon in the john, Jerry finds out just how ultra–feisty he is. He's challenged to a fight, at guess what time, in the parking lot. As Jerry wracks his brain for every way possible out of the match, he's foiled at every turn, managing to get in trouble with school security, the principal, various teachers, and his best friend. Meanwhile, he's tortured by analogies of his imminent doom which lurk in every class. In science, an explicit depiction of a cricket being eaten by a predator ignites Jerry's fear. In history, the teacher lectures on Hector being dragged by Achilles chariot and then mutilated by wild dogs. Even his friends, two would–be UCLA film students, are more interested in filming the fight than helping him. The day from Hell never lets up for poor Jerry, and the incident in the school store, which Jerry has trashed, elicits the comment from one teacher, "Whoever did this should be plucked out of this school like a burgeoning cancer deep inside the colon." The relentless nature of Jerry's tortures is helped along by the souped–up direction by Spielberg protégé Joanou and the ever-wandering camera work of Sonnenfeld.

# The Toxic Avenger

**(1989) 90m**
Andree Maranda, Mitchell Cohen, Pat Ryan, Jr., Jennifer Babtist,
Robert Prichard, Cindy Manion, Gary Schneider, Mark Torgl
**D:** Michael Herz
**P:** Lloyd Kaufman Michael Herz
**C:** James London
**S:** Joe Ritter

Spoof on sci–fi, horror, and filmmaking in general is for those who like a little comedy with their gratuitous violence. Series established Troma Pictures as caterers to the very lowbrow and helped put Jersey back on the map with its own superhero, however slimy. Tromaville is the home of Melvin, a 98-lb. nerd who works as the mop boy at the Tromaville Health Club. Melvin's mere presence irks the local gang of bullies led by Bobo, who, when they're not pumping iron or lifting weights, are engaging in their favorite pastime of running over innocent people with their car, earning points for difficulty. Because Melvin is ugly, nerdy, skinny, stupid, and lives in Tromaville, Bobo's gang decides to play a practical joke on him which involves a pink tutu and a farm animal. The joke traumatizes poor Melvin, so much so that he jumps out of window and lands into a vat of chemical waste. Melvin emerges from the waste a changed man, to say the least. He becomes a lumbering, blood-thirsty hulk with one very lazy eye. Banished from his ma's home, he makes his new home at the local waste dump. In his endeavors to fight crime and seek revenge, Melvin, now Toxie, earns a reputation as the "monster hero" and becomes the idol of misguided Jersey children. Fearing that he may be the monster's next victim, the corrupt mayor wants Toxie dead. Action, adventure and even romance await as Toxie meets and falls in love with a blind blond bimbo. Enhanced by purposely bad acting, occasionally tongue-in-cheek cult fave is tasteless on every count. Followed by not one but two sequels with even more grotesque violence.

# They Call Me Bruce?

**(1982) 88m PG**
Johnny Yune, Margaux Hemingway, Ralph Mauro, Pam Huntington
**D:** Eliot Hong **P:** Eliot Hong **C:** Robert Roth
**S:** Tim Clawson **M:** Tommy Vig

Martial arts parody has Bruce Lee look-a-like Yune as a pasta spinner working for a bunch of Italian mobsters, who, like the title says, call him Bruce. The similarities end with his looks, however, as Bruce is faster with his tongue than with his hands ("He can't even chop liver," one mobster cracks). But Bruce of course fantasizes that he is Bruce Lee, even signing up for kung–fu classes. He is advised by the kung–fu master, "It takes patience—it's all mental." "My father was a mental patient," replies Bruce, a remark that only an amateur screenwriter could convincingly write. Although a complete martial arts moron, Bruce is reassessed as a kung–fu expert by his bosses after he accidentally knocks out a robber. They send him on a dangerous cocaine delivery to New York. Bruce, however, thinks he's delivering his secret flour for pasta noodles. Soon Bruce is a marked man, though he manages to avoid most every fight with fast–talking and by following the advice his grandfather in China gave him: "If you must fight, grandson, fight dirty. Kick 'em in the groin." The movie opens with granddad on his deathbed advising young Bruce, "Remember, grandson, the most important thing in life is not money...it's broads!" We're still looking for a fortune cookie with that little message. In the end, Bruce does manage to find love in a karate–chopping Mafia moll (Hemingway, who must have been looking for work). The stereotypes and stale jokes fly faster than a Kawasaki, as *Bruce* spoofs *The Godfather* and the *Kung–Fu* television series, as well as *Saturday Night Fever, Rocky,* James Bond flicks, and even the Life cereal commercial (remember Mikey?). Stand–up comedian Yune remarkably seems more like a stand–up comedian than actor (well, it works for Jerry Seinfeld) with plenty of one–liners that will make you laugh and roll your eyes at the same time. Sequel *They Still Call Me Bruce* is substandard in comparison, which is all you need to know.

# Queen of Outer Space

**(1958) 80m**
Zsa Zsa Gabor, Eric Fleming, Laurie Mitchell, Patrick Waltz,
Paul Birch, Lisa Davis
**D:** Edward Bernds
**P:** Ben Schwalb
**C:** William P. Whitley
**S:** Charles Beaumont, Ben Hecht
**M:** Marlin Skiles

In one of the most hilariously camp movies ever made, a spaceship crew lands on Venus and finds the planet inhabited by a group of beautiful babes sporting miniskirts, boots, and lipstick. Captain Fleming, leader of the spacemen, falls for Gabor (Hungarian accent and all), but problems arise because the Queen of Venus (Mitchell) has issued a no–men–allowed rule. While space cadets crack chauvinistic jokes about the vampy Venusian vixens, the Queen decides to destroy Earth using her Beta Disintegrator Ray. Although there are a few lame attempts at humor, the laughs really come when the cast plays it straight. If some of the sets and props look familiar, it's because they were recycled from other sci-fi films. The nifty costumes, ray guns, and forest setting are from *Forbidden Planet;* other sets and a giant spider were left over from *World Without End;* and the rocket ship is from *Flight to Mars.* It may be hard to believe, but this notorious sci-fi cheapie is based on a story by Ben Hecht.

---

### Zsa Zsa, Dahling

| | |
|---|---|
| Arrivederci, Baby! (1966) | Frankenstein's Great Aunt Tillie (1983) |
| Every Girl Should Have One (1978) | Pee Wee's Playhouse Christmas Special (1988) |

# Amazon Women on the Moon

**(1987) 85m R**
Rosanna Arquette, Ralph Bellamy, Carrie Fisher, Griffin Dunne,
Steve Guttenberg, Michelle Pfeiffer, B.B. King, Steve Allen
**D:** Joe Dante, John Landis, Carl Gottleib, Peter Horton, Robert Weiss
**P:** Robert K. Weiss
**C:** Daniel Pearl
**S:** Michael Barrie
**M:** Marshall Harvey

Yet another plotless, loosely constructed media spoof. This one depicts the programming of a slipshod television station as it crams weird commercials and shorts around a comical '50s sci–fi flick. The title piece is a clever mix of '50s cheapie sci–fi-complete with a moon expedition. The music adds to the scene as it parodies the period too. Other highlights include the skits "Son of the Invisible Man," "Video Pirates," and the Dante-directed "Damaged Lives/Sex Madness." There's even a funny Siskel/Ebert parody and Henry Silva doing a side-splitting takeoff of Leonard Nimoy and *In Search Of . . .* This low-budget piece of insanity lingered on the shelf for nearly a year before receiving a theatrical release, and is now finally finding new life on video.

---

### Director Joe Dante in the Hot Seat

| | |
|---|---|
| The Burbs (1989) | Innerspace (1987) |
| Gremlins(1984) | Twilight Zone: The Movie (1983) |
| Gremlins 2: The New Batch (1990) | |

*Life in outer space isn't so bad, after all.*

**R**esist the temptation or you may end up like Pete and Mary and Ken.

*Doctor (Paul Bartel) in the ominous last line of the movie*

# Beverly Hillbillies

**(1993) 93m PG**

Jim Varney, Erika Eleniak, Diedrich Bader, Cloris Leachman,
Dabney Coleman, Lily Tomlin, Lea Thompson, Rob Schneider
**D:** Penelope Spheeris
**P:** Ian Bryce, Penelope Spheeris
**C:** Robert Brinkmann
**S:** Jim Fisher, Lawrence Konner, Mark Rosenthal, Jim Staahl
**M:** Lalo Schifrin

Hear the sounds of the twanging banjo, see the old jalopy putting down a tree–lined avenue in posh Beverly Hills toting a very out–of–place, motley crew. Yes, Jed and all his kin are back and this time they're in the fee–tures. If you're looking for a heapin' helpin' of roadkill stew and a down–home hoedown, this is the movie to serve it up 'cause it's even dumber than the classic TV sitcom. Varney doubles as the good–hearted Jed and Leachman as the forever crusty Granny. The clan enters town puttering down the freeway, mistaking another driver's middle finger salute as an authentic "Beverly Hills howdy." They then proceed to happily bid hello in the native way to all the other passing cars. This is just the beginning of the fish–out–of–water syndrome that the Clampetts encounter. Jethro (Bader) is trying to find a suitable bride for his lonely but obviously eligible (he's a billionaire!) bachelor uncle. In walks underhanded gold digger Thompson, posing as a French governess who seems to be the perfect role model for daughter Elly May (Eleniak). But watch out Clampetts—this pretty little thing and her sleazy banker boyfriend (Schneider) are closing in for the kill. The cast is rounded out cleverly with Coleman as the uppity Mr. Drysdale and Tomlin as his prim and proper assistant, Miss Hathaway, who still has that unexplainable crush on Jethro. Surprise cameos by Zsa Zsa Gabor (Miss Beverly Hills herself), Dolly Parton, and Buddy Ebsen (the original Jed) reprising another familiar TV icon of his, Barnaby Jones, add to the lowbrow fun.

*Howdy, ya'll!*

# Cabin Boy

**(1994) 80m PG-13**

Chris Elliott, Ann Magnuson, Ritch Brinkley, James Gammon,
Brian Doyle-Murray, Russ Tamblyn, Brion James, Ricki Lake,
Bob Elliott, Earl Hofert (David Letterman)
**D:** Adam Resnick
**P:** Tim Burton
**C:** Steve Yaconelli
**S:** Adam Resnick
**M:** Steven Bartek

Welcome to the longest 80 minutes in recent cinema history, a silly fest that occasionally works but gets points for simply existing (what were they thinking?). Taking the helm at last place in this boatload of idiot's delights is not the worst movie of all time, but it's certainly up there with the most inane, unredeemable Hollywood efforts ever, which makes it the perfect choice to close the list. Fancy lad Elliott accidentally boards the wrong boat and finds himself as the new cabin boy for a crew of rude, smelly, obnoxious sailors. What follows is a surreal blend of fish-out-of-water comedy and fantasy that for the most part doesn't work, probably due to the lack of a script. Humor is mostly derived from intentionally cheesy sets coupled with a plot that's obviously not meant to be taken seriously. Highlights include Elliott's show-biz friends that show up briefly; look for Letterman as an old salt trying to sell his monkey, Lake as part of the ship, and real life dad Bob Elliot (of Bob and Ray fame) as the fancy lad's father. Surprisingly produced by Tim Burton, who must have had a vision of the boat in a bathtub and was able somehow to transfer that image to screen intact. At least Letterman got some laughs out of his role during the Academy Awards show—he played a video with an array of big–wig actor buddies trying out his line to hock a stuffed monkey.

*The gang from "Porky's."*

## Porky's Gets Panned:

"One of those movies that makes you weep for the state
of the contemporary cinema—and, even more, for the
gullibility of the public that pays to see it."

*Margaret Hinxman*, Daily Mail *(well, it ain't no* "Godfather")

# Ernest Goes to Camp

**(1987) 92m PG**
Jim Varney, Victoria Racimo, John Vernon, Iron Eyes Cody, Lyle Alzado,
Gailard Sartain, Daniel Butler, Hakeem Abdul-Samad
**D:** John R. Cherry III
**P:** Stacy Williams
**C:** Harry Mathias, Jim May
**S:** John R. Cherry III
**M:** Shane Keister

To choose just one Ernest movie from the collected work is a tough job, knowwhatImean? Pea-brained pitchman Ernest P. Worrell stars in the first of the sometimes dreadful but always compellingly dumb series of movies capitalizing on the popularity of Varney's commercial character. Ernest wants to be a counselor in this summer camp farce, and instead lands the position of custodial engineer. As luck would have it, one of the counselors is injured and Ernest does indeed get a chance to advise the biggest delinquents of the camp, who waste no time in getting down to the business of harassing their less-than-genius mentor. Enter bad-guy Bronk Stinson (Alzado) who uses Varney as his unwitting flunky to persuade camp owner Old Indian Chief (Cody) to shut down the place and sign away his land rights. Heroic Ernest must prevent this travesty and leads the misguided youths in an all-out battle, complete with flaming arrows and snapping turtles, to save Camp Kikakee. Check your brain at the door and enjoy mild chuckle spasms throughout.

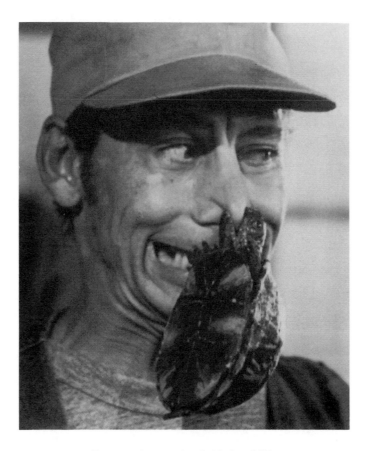

*Ernest getting acquainted with the wildlife.*

## All-Out Ernest

| | |
|---|---|
| Slam Dunk Ernest (1995) | Ernest Goes to Jail (1990) |
| Ernest Rides Again (1993) | Ernest Saves Christmas (1988) |
| Ernest Scared Stupid(1991) | |

# Airheads

**1994 PG-13**

Brendan Fraser, Steve Buscemi, Adam Sandler, Chris Farley,
Michael McKean, Judd Nelson, Joe Mantegna, Michael Richards,
Ernie Hudson, Nina Siemaszko, John Melendez, Amy Locane
**D:** Michael Lehmann
**P:** Mark Burg, Robert Simonds
**C:** John Schwartzman
**S:** Rich Wilkes
**M:** Carter Burwell

Anarchy and rock-n-roll are blended into this farce that attempts the heretofore untried compound of *Wayne's World* and *Dog Day Afternoon*. Three members (Fraser, Buscemi, and Sandler) from a basement rock band called the Lone Rangers are determined to get their demo tape heard on the radio. But asking nicely doesn't seem to work, so in their own bumbling manner, they hold up a local radio station, using water pistols to take hostages of the surprised star DJ and stuffy program manager. As the hostage situation is recorded on the air, the event snowballs into a media circus. The Lone Rangers become the darlings of an adoring metalhead crowd short on brains but long on gusto gathering outside the radio station. Somehow, mere plot summary (or for that matter, an autographed copy of the script) will not suffice to explain how the Three Stooges of rock-n-roll become a triumphant underdog symbol for the suppressed youth of America. Borrowing the classic "Attica, Attica" scene from *Dog Day Afternoon,* Fraser riles the crowd by chanting "Rodney King." Occasionally deserted by the writing and directing team, but supported by a cast rich with subversive comedic talents. Mantegna contributes a hip performance as DJ Ian, while McKean is a hoot as the weasely program director. Comes complete with a kickin' soundtrack supplied by White Zombie and The Galactic Cowboys. Don't try to watch this and do your doctoral dissertation at the same time.

*Chazz (Fraser) and Rex (Buscemi) give police their list of demands,
which includes the latest Barry Manilow release.*

## Behind every great script, there's hard-earned experience:

Screenwriter Wilkes actually tried to sneak into Capitol
Records before he wrote the scene where Chazz does the
same thing—except instead of meeting a top exec, Wilkes
was brutalized and thrown out by security.

# Rosencrantz & Guildenstern Are Dead

**(1990) 118m PG**
Gary Oldman, Tim Roth, Richard Dreyfuss, Iain Glen, Joanna Roth,
Joanna Miles, Ian Richardson, Donald Sumpter
**D:** Tom Stoppard
**P:** Emmanuel Azenburg, Michael Brandman
**C:** Peter Biziou
**S:** Tom Stoppard, based on his play
**M:** Brian Gulland, Stanley Myers, Graham Preskett

Heads, you'll like this movie. Tails, you won't (now you'll have to see it just to get this reference). Although playwright Stoppard adapted his absurdist 1967 play for film with less success than he had on the stage, it's still a worthy view. Two confused minor characters of Shakespeare's *Hamlet* squabble rhetorically and completely miss the plot that's tightening fatally around them. Oldman and Roth are hilarious as the dim-witted duo who try to make sense out of their senseless situation. One of their best moments is a verbal tennis match, a gem since neither could be mistaken for a genius. Dreyfuss, as a menacing thespian, tries to hip them to their hopeless circumstances to an amusing conclusion.

**Rosencrantz: Is there a choice?**

**Guildenstern: Is there a God?**

**Rosencrantz: Foul! No non sequiturs.**

*R & G explain one rule of
their verbal tennis match called "Questions."*

*No noose is good noose!*

**Guildenstern:** You're tumblers, then?

**Head Player:** We can give you a tumble, if that is your taste...and times being what they are.

**Rosencrantz:** What exactly is it you do?

**Head Player:** We keep to our usual stuff, more or less, only inside out. We do on stage the things that are supposed to happen off, which is a kind of integrity if you look on every exit as an entrance (slight pause) somewhere else.

*Richard Dreyfuss confuses R & G*

# Police Academy

**(1984) 96m R**
Steve Guttenberg, Kim Cattrall, Bubba Smith, George Gaynes,
Michael Winslow, Leslie Easterbrook, Georgina Spelvin, Debralee Scott
**D:** Hugh Wilson
**P:** Paul Maslansky
**C:** Michael D. Margulies
**S:** Neal Israel, Pat Proft, Hugh Wilson
**M:** Robert Folk

Does for the police department what *Marathon Man* did for dentistry, elevating the stature of *Car 54, Where Are You?* in the process. A big-city police department needs more recruits, so what do they do? Fix it so that just about anyone can be a cop, including normally unemployable actors. Soon the typical band of law-enforcement misfit wannabes are in training to be the city's finest. Guttenberg, as lead flunky who wants to up the academy, has the best bit with his demonstration of proper parking technique. As the dense commandant overlooking it all, Gaynes finds financial security above and beyond *Punky Brewster*. Bailey, as the lead nemesis, plays and encounters a real horse's ass. Broad blue humor and slapstick unsupported by much of a script is probably best appreciated by individuals wanting to get in touch with their inner adolescent. With all the delightful sequels, you'll spend days slapping your head muttering, "I could've written this!"

> ## The academy is taking all kinds today.
> ## Anybody can get in. Even you.
>
> *Captain Reed (Ross)*
> *speaks to Carey Mahoney (Guttenberg).*

*Cmdt. Lassard separates two of his newest recruits, Fackler and Zed, in "Police Academy 3."*

---

### Freeze! Or They'll Shoot!

Police Academy 2: Their First Assignment (1985)

Police Academy 3: Back in Training (1986)

Police Academy 4: Citizens on Patrol (1987)

Police Academy 5: Assignment Miami Beach (1988)

Police Academy 6: City Under Siege (1989)

# Coneheads

**(1993) 86m PG**
Dan Aykroyd, Jane Curtin, Laraine Newman, Jason Alexander,
Michelle Burke, Chris Farley, Michael Richards, Michael McKeon,
David Spade, Jan Hooks, Julia Sweeney, Lisa Jane Persky
**D:** Steven Barron

Stranded on Earth, Aykroyd and Curtin reprise their roles as Beldar and Prymaat, the elders of the family from France (but really aliens from Remulak) who are just trying to fit in. Stuffed with cast members from *Saturday Night Live* past and present (and maybe future, as Aykroyd's toddler daughter Danielle makes her film debut), the comedy all-stars provide the film with a lift. Newman, who created the role of daughter Connie, appears as Beldar's sister, while Burke takes over as the teen. Farley is the love interest of Connie and finds himself astounded at the furious speed at which she consumes submarine sandwiches on their first date (he thought only his mother could eat a sub like that). The audience even gets a glimpse of Remulak itself when the family is rescued but finds they no longer fit into their native home. Fans of the original *SNL* skit will enjoy reminiscing over the popular '70s comic shtick, even though it would have done better about a decade earlier. Others will enjoy the parade of recent *SNL* regulars. McKean and Spade steal the show as the two immigration officials out to expose the true identity of the secretive family. They even go as far as to disguise themselves as Jehovah's Witnesses. Promoted with the line, "As much pleasure as can be obtained with your lower extremities still garbed."

*Bald is beautiful.*

# Return of the Living Dead

**(1985) 90m R**

Clu Gulager, James Karen, Linnea Quigley, Don Calfa, Jewel Shepard
**D:** Dan O'Bannon
**P:** Tom Fox
**C:** Jules Brenner
**S:** Dan O' Bannon
**M:** Matt Clifford

An often clever and scary combination of sequel–to and spoof–of Romero's classic horror film. Poisonous gas seeps into a small town and has the natural effect of reviving the inhabitants of the local cemetery. The once *dead* dead now join the ranks of the living dead and raise havoc with the living in their pursuit of eating brains, brains, and still more brains. Punctuated by punk music, exaggerated gore, and outright silliness (Karen has a hilarious scene where he aides in the destruction of a zombie in a warehouse), it's hard to believe that director O'Bannon wrote the creepier and more serious *Alien*. But doubt no further and watch as O'Bannon duplicates one of the eerie scenes from that sci–fi classic by having an embalmer question a mutilated zombie lying on his table, asking the somewhat decomposed somnabulist why zombies eat brains. The movie even begins with the tongue–in–cheek disclaimer, "the events depicted are true." A rash of bad acting by teens who play characters named Trash and Suicide places the film in its true perspective, an outrageous spoof on the living dead sub–genre.

> ## I love you—I want to eat your brains!
>
> *Thom Matthews, a walking corpse who can't decide what he really wants from his living girlfriend, Beverly Randolph*

# House Party

**(1990) 100m**

Christopher Reid, Christopher Martin, Martin Lawrence, Tisha Campbell,
Paul Anthony, A.J. Johnson, Full Force, Robin Harris, John Witherspoon

**D:** Reginald Hudlin
**S:** Reginald Hudlin
**P:** Warrington Hudlin
**C:** Peter Deming
**M:** Marcus Miller

Energetic and silly hip–hop romp showcases rap group Kid 'n' Play in a low-budget box-office hit expanded from writer/director Reggie Hudlin's Harvard short. With a typical *Leave It to Beaver* plot, tower-haired Kid wants to go to his friend Play's ultimate house party. But after a fight in the school cafeteria, he's grounded by his frustrated dad (the late Robin Harris). Kid is not one to let an opportunity of meeting cute girls and a chance at rapping on the microphone escape him, so he sneaks out the house past his sleeping father (enjoying a dose of *Dolemite*). Getting to the party becomes complicated as three hoods (Full Force) hound him, while the cops chase them all. Kid temporarily stops off at a more mature benefit d-jayed by a bored George Clinton. Meanwhile, Dad is awake and stalking the neighborhood, cursing his kid Kid for having a head like an "ol' tree stump." At the house party, the action is electric as hips gyrate and hands wave in the air with some great dance sequences and rap numbers. Martin Lawrence displays early comedic promise as the d.j. who badly wants a date, but whose present girlfriend Hallie (as in halitosis) stands in his way. The further adventures of Kid 'n' Play are followed in two lesser sequels, as the writing/producing/directing Hudlins departed for the animated *Bebe's Kids* (written by Robin Harris) and *Boomerang* with Eddie Murphy. In *House Party II,* Kid 'n' Play hold a pajama jammy jam to raise college tuition. And it's more diminishing returns as *House Party III* focuses on Kid's engagement and subsequent bachelor party.

# Saturday the 14th

**(1981) 91m PG**

Richard Benjamin, Paula Prentiss, Severn Darden, Kevin Brando,
Jeffrey Tambor, Kari Michaelson, Nancy Lee Andrews, Rosemary DeCamp
**D:** Howard R. Cohen
**P:** Julie Corman
**S:** Howard R. Cohen, Jeff Begun

A parody not, as the title suggests, of modern slasher films, but of the kinder, gentler monster movies of yore. This one's about a family inheriting a haunted mansion. Prentiss and Benjamin, who are also off-screen husband and wife, play the unfortunate couple, with Brando as their son. Brando manages to evoke various vampires and assorted monsters who begin to make their cameo appearances. Soon the family is engulfed in ghouls who are there seeking the hidden, ancient "Book of Evil." Lots of good gags and cast keep it entertaining and fun. Followed by *Saturday the 14th Strikes Back,* a weak sequel which introduces another family in another haunted mansion but without the benefit of a strong cast to make it work.

---

### Equally Cheesy Monster Spoofs

Hell Comes to Frogtown (1988)   Strange Invaders (1983)

Repossessed (1990)                    Teenage Exorcist (1993)

---

*Oh, the life of a monster—Calgon, take me away!*

## Completely useless *Saturday the 14th* trivia

*or How to Tie A Really Bad Movie to a Respectable TV Program:*

Ray Walston, who starred in the Saturday sequel, finally won an Emmy award for his work on the TV series *Picket Fences*, after 60 years of television work.

# Major League

**(1989) 106m R**

Tom Berenger, Charlie Sheen, Corbin Bernsen, Margaret Whitton, James
Gammon, Rene Russo, Wesley Snipes, Charles Cyphers, Dennis Haysbert,
Bob Uecker

**D:** David S. Ward
**P:** Chris Chesser, Irby Smith
**C:** Reynaldo Villalobos
**S:** David S. Ward
**M:** James Newton Howard

Heeere's the pitch. America's favorite pastime may not be recovering well from the recent strike, but baseball movies are always
a hit. Throw in some comedy and you've got a home run. Rich-
bitch owner of the Cleveland Indians (back when they were perpetual underachievers) has losing (and moving to Florida) in
mind when she assembles a team of scrubs—until the guys find
out and rally into champions. You've seen this motley crew of
clichéd baseball chuckleheads before—the wise but washed-up
veteran catcher, the egomaniac superstar, the superstitious
voodoo worshipper, the Bible-thumper, and the wild young
pitcher with potential—but never with so many laughs. Sheen is
especially fun as the ex-con rock and roll hurler ("What league
were you in last year?" "California Penal.") whose control problems earn him the tag "Wild Thing" and make him a fan favorite.
The boys go from last to first, in improbable fashion. Stretched
to extra innings with a sequel, *Major League 2* (1994) including
basically the same plot and cast, but Omar Epps pinch-hits for
Snipes. New clichés include a catcher who can't throw the ball
back to the pitcher and the former "Wild Thing" going corporate.

*Third baseman Bernsen shows pitcher Sheen what a baseball looks like.*

**W**omen! You can't live without em,
and they can't pee standin' up.

*Rube Baker on relationships in "Major League 2."*

# Zorro, the Gay Blade

**(1981) 96m PG**
George Hamilton, Lauren Hutton, Brenda Vaccaro, Ron Leibman,
Donovan Scott, James Booth
**D:** Peter Medak
**P:** Greg Alt, Don Moriarty
**C:** John A. Alonzo
**S:** Hal Dresner
**M:** Ian Fraser

Hamilton follows his first successful spoof, *Love at First Bite*,
with this affectionate send–up of the legendary Latin swashbuckler. In a dual role that must have severely stretched his thespian
talents, Hamilton is the gallant swordsman Zorro (of '60s television fame) and his Liberace–like gay twin brother. It seems that
Don Diego Vega (Hamilton), son of Zorro, is spurred to take up
daddy's mask and sword when a cruel tyrant, Alcalde (Leibman
in an over-the-top, at the top-of-his-lungs bit), terrorizes local
villagers. After Zorro is injured, his long–lost twin brother,
Bunny Wigglesworth, suddenly arrives from England and
pledges to help. While Zorro has a flair for the dramatic, Bunny
has a flair for fashion, changing the basic black costume to more
colorful attire. His motto is, "There is no shame in being poor,
only in dressing poor." With this flamboyant assistant, the handsome hunk beats the bad guy and gets the gorgeous girl, Hutton.
While the gags eventually run dry, Hamilton, with ham firmly on
wry, provides an inspired parody of the masked man in black.

*George Hamilton camping it up to the hilt.*

# Brain Donors

**(1992) 79m PG**
John Turturro, Bob Nelson, Mel Smith, Nancy Marchand, Teri Copley,
George De La Pena, Spike Alexander, John Savident
**D:** Dennis Dugan
**P:** Gil Netter, James D. Brubaker
**C:** David M. Walsh
**S:** Pat Proft
**M:** Ira Newborn

With executive producers David and Jerry Zucker lending their names to the producer credits (and presumedly some bucks) and cohort Pat Proft doing the words, *Brain Donors* is *Problem Child* director Dugan's homage to the Marx Brothers and *A Night at the Opera*, with a fair bit of Loony Tunes madness thrown in for good measure. Bursting with silly repartee in the manner of classic Groucho, a nonsensical plot involving a ballet company, and sight gags galore (many of them revolving around the hidden assets of Harpo mimic Nelson's coat of many surprises), it's still surprisingly flat at times. But what the hell, they really try (particularly Turturro in his Groucho turn), and it's only 79 minutes long! As Flakfizer remarks early on, "Nothing like the thrill of spending an evening watching a bunch of anorexics leaping around guys with bulging genitals." What there is of a plot revolves around desire of newly widowed and fabulously rich Lillian Oglethorpe (Marchand) to create a ballet company in memory of her late husband. Though opposed by stuffy lawyer Laslo (Savident), sleazy lawyer Roland T. Flakfizer (Turturro) and his two zany cohorts (Harpo and Chico) are there to help, or at least to make a quick buck. "Lillian, I have a dream," says Flakfizer at the reading of the will. "We'll bring in a whole new breed of ballet goer with innovative giveaways—leotard night, wet tutu competitions—and we'll be the first company to perform ballet for the hard of hearing: we'll have the ballerinas wearing wooden shoes!" The movie even ventures to restage the famous crowded stateroom scene from *A Night at the Opera*, showing at the very least guts if not skill, and in Dugan's case, we're pretty sure it's

*John Turturro points the finger at fellow donor.*

not *great* skill. Fast-paced and broadly surreal, with Turturro continually sputtering lines and lots of bad jokes, it culminates with a *Swan Lake* in which the dying swan receives CPR, a giant duck joins the dancers, dancing duck hunters and a pack of hounds invade, and the duck is shot dead. Annoying claymation credits by Will Vinton accompanied by annoying theme music by Ira Newborn open and close at length, making the movie several minutes shorter than the 79 minutes credited. And yes, the title is a complete mystery; originally it was entitled *Lame Ducks*.

# Caveman

**(1981) 91m PG**

Ringo Starr, Dennis Quaid, Shelley Long, Jack Gilford, John Matuszak,
Barbara Bach, Cork Hubbert, Mark King, Paco Morayta, Evan Kim,
Ed Greenberg, Carl Lumbly, Jack Scalici
**D:** Carl Gottlieb
**P:** David Foster, Lawrence Turman
**C:** Alan Hume
**S:** Rudy DeLuca, Carl Gottlieb
**M:** Lalo Schifrin

*Atouk aloona Lana. Lana aloona Tonda. Tala aloona Atouk.*
With a script of only 15 English words, you'll have to master
cavespeak quickly to appreciate *Caveman,* undoubtedly the
dumbest movie ever set in One Zillion B.C. (October 9th to be
exact). Okay, so it's not exactly a classic, but this stone age spoof
earns nomination for appropriately casting the Funny Beatle as
Atouk, your average prehistoric guy. Atouk's in love with the lus-
cious, well–oiled, fur bikini–clad Lana (Bach), who provides
proof that ancient women inexplicably had access to Nair. But
Lana belongs to the humongous and very hairy Tonda
(Matuszak), and Atouk's attempts to gain her affection (or at
least get some *zug–zug*) get him bounced from the cave. Atouk
meets up with cave buddy Lar (Quaid) and becomes the leader of
an outcast group, including the lovely Tala (Long).  Together
they search for *ool* (food), get caught in a nearby Ice Age, fight
off dinosaurs that look like lame Godzilla movie rejects, and
launch an attack on Tonda and his simian crew.  If nothing else,
*Caveman* proves that gags with a decidedly scatological bent are
indeed the oldest jokes in the world.  No matter—despite lots of
gross–out moments, classic slapstick rules. Ringo and company
even invent (what else?) rock 'n' roll in one of the niftier scenes.
So relax those overworked synapses and enjoy a goofy journey
into the primitive past.

*Starr rescues wife Bach from the clutches of Dennis Quaid.*

## Cavespeak to English Dictionary:

zug-zug = sex

ool = food

oweey = fire

Abana abou attoma = call my agent, we'll do lunch

# Three O'Clock High

**(1987) PG 97m**
Casey Siemaszko, Anne Ryan, Stacey Glick, Jonathan Wise,
Richard Tyson, Jeffrey Tambor, Liza Morrow, John P. Ryan, Philip Baker Hall
**D:** Phil Joanou
**C:** Barry Sonnenfeld
**W:** Richard Christian Matheson, Thomas Szollosi

Appropriating *Risky Business* (complete with ethereal music by Tangerine Dream) and *Ferris Bueller's Day Off, Three O'Clock High* is a worthy entry in the hell high school category. Siemaszko (complete with bratty sister) is the cute, kinda nerdy high school journalist Jerry Mitchell, who wakes up late on the first day of school, foreshadowing the kind of day it's going to be for our plucky protagonist. His first assignment: a scoop on the new kid in school, whose sullied reputation as a homicidal bully and troublemaker precedes him. Buddy Ravell (Tyson) turns out to be just that, and after a not–so–friendly confrontation with the goon in the john, Jerry finds out just how ultra–feisty he is. He's challenged to a fight, at guess what time, in the parking lot. As Jerry wracks his brain for every way possible out of the match, he's foiled at every turn, managing to get in trouble with school security, the principal, various teachers, and his best friend. Meanwhile, he's tortured by analogies of his imminent doom which lurk in every class. In science, an explicit depiction of a cricket being eaten by a predator ignites Jerry's fear. In history, the teacher lectures on Hector being dragged by Achilles chariot and then mutilated by wild dogs. Even his friends, two would–be UCLA film students, are more interested in filming the fight than helping him. The day from Hell never lets up for poor Jerry, and the incident in the school store, which Jerry has trashed, elicits the comment from one teacher, "Whoever did this should be plucked out of this school like a burgeoning cancer deep inside the colon." The relentless nature of Jerry's tortures is helped along by the souped–up direction by Spielberg protégé Joanou and the ever-wandering camera work of Sonnenfeld.

# The Toxic Avenger

**(1989) 90m**
Andree Maranda, Mitchell Cohen, Pat Ryan, Jr., Jennifer Babtist,
Robert Prichard, Cindy Manion, Gary Schneider, Mark Torgl
**D:** Michael Herz
**P:** Lloyd Kaufman Michael Herz
**C:** James London
**S:** Joe Ritter

Spoof on sci–fi, horror, and filmmaking in general is for those
who like a little comedy with their gratuitous violence. Series
established Troma Pictures as caterers to the very lowbrow and
helped put Jersey back on the map with its own superhero, however slimy. Tromaville is the home of Melvin, a 98-lb. nerd who
works as the mop boy at the Tromaville Health Club. Melvin's
mere presence irks the local gang of bullies led by Bobo, who,
when they're not pumping iron or lifting weights, are engaging
in their favorite pastime of running over innocent people with
their car, earning points for difficulty. Because Melvin is ugly,
nerdy, skinny, stupid, and lives in Tromaville, Bobo's gang
decides to play a practical joke on him which involves a pink tutu
and a farm animal. The joke traumatizes poor Melvin, so much
so that he jumps out of window and lands into a vat of chemical
waste. Melvin emerges from the waste a changed man, to say the
least. He becomes a lumbering, blood-thirsty hulk with one very
lazy eye. Banished from his ma's home, he makes his new home
at the local waste dump. In his endeavors to fight crime and seek
revenge, Melvin, now Toxie, earns a reputation as the "monster
hero" and becomes the idol of misguided Jersey children. Fearing that he may be the monster's next victim, the corrupt mayor
wants Toxie dead. Action, adventure and even romance await as
Toxie meets and falls in love with a blind blond bimbo. Enhanced
by purposely bad acting, occasionally tongue-in-cheek cult fave
is tasteless on every count. Followed by not one but two sequels
with even more grotesque violence.

# They Call Me Bruce?

**(1982) 88m PG**
Johnny Yune, Margaux Hemingway, Ralph Mauro, Pam Huntington
**D:** Eliot Hong **P:** Eliot Hong **C:** Robert Roth
**S:** Tim Clawson **M:** Tommy Vig

Martial arts parody has Bruce Lee look-a-like Yune as a pasta spin-ner working for a bunch of Italian mobsters, who, like the title says, call him Bruce. The similarities end with his looks, however, as Bruce is faster with his tongue than with his hands ("He can't even chop liver," one mobster cracks). But Bruce of course fanta-sizes that he is Bruce Lee, even signing up for kung–fu classes. He is advised by the kung–fu master, "It takes patience—it's all men-tal." "My father was a mental patient," replies Bruce, a remark that only an amateur screenwriter could convincingly write. Although a complete martial arts moron, Bruce is reassessed as a kung–fu expert by his bosses after he accidentally knocks out a robber. They send him on a dangerous cocaine delivery to New York. Bruce, however, thinks he's delivering his secret flour for pasta noodles. Soon Bruce is a marked man, though he manages to avoid most every fight with fast–talking and by following the advice his grand-father in China gave him: "If you must fight, grandson, fight dirty. Kick 'em in the groin." The movie opens with granddad on his deathbed advising young Bruce, "Remember, grandson, the most important thing in life is not money...it's broads!" We're still look-ing for a fortune cookie with that little message. In the end, Bruce does manage to find love in a karate–chopping Mafia moll (Hem-ingway, who must have been looking for work). The stereotypes and stale jokes fly faster than a Kawasaki, as *Bruce* spoofs *The Godfather* and the *Kung–Fu* television series, as well as *Saturday Night Fever, Rocky,* James Bond flicks, and even the Life cereal commercial (remember Mikey?). Stand–up comedian Yune remarkably seems more like a stand–up comedian than actor (well, it works for Jerry Seinfeld) with plenty of one–liners that will make you laugh and roll your eyes at the same time. Sequel *They Still Call Me Bruce* is substandard in comparison, which is all you need to know.

# Queen of Outer Space

**(1958) 80m**
Zsa Zsa Gabor, Eric Fleming, Laurie Mitchell, Patrick Waltz,
Paul Birch, Lisa Davis
**D:** Edward Bernds
**P:** Ben Schwalb
**C:** William P. Whitley
**S:** Charles Beaumont, Ben Hecht
**M:** Marlin Skiles

In one of the most hilariously camp movies ever made, a space-ship crew lands on Venus and finds the planet inhabited by a group of beautiful babes sporting miniskirts, boots, and lipstick. Captain Fleming, leader of the spacemen, falls for Gabor (Hungarian accent and all), but problems arise because the Queen of Venus (Mitchell) has issued a no–men–allowed rule. While space cadets crack chauvinistic jokes about the vampy Venusian vixens, the Queen decides to destroy Earth using her Beta Disintegrator Ray. Although there are a few lame attempts at humor, the laughs really come when the cast plays it straight. If some of the sets and props look familiar, it's because they were recycled from other sci-fi films. The nifty costumes, ray guns, and forest setting are from *Forbidden Planet;* other sets and a giant spider were left over from *World Without End;* and the rocket ship is from *Flight to Mars.* It may be hard to believe, but this notorious sci-fi cheapie is based on a story by Ben Hecht.

---

### Zsa Zsa, Dahling

| | |
|---|---|
| Arrivederci, Baby! (1966) | Frankenstein's Great Aunt Tillie (1983) |
| Every Girl Should Have One (1978) | Pee Wee's Playhouse Christmas Special (1988) |

# Amazon Women on the Moon

**(1987) 85m R**
Rosanna Arquette, Ralph Bellamy, Carrie Fisher, Griffin Dunne,
Steve Guttenberg, Michelle Pfeiffer, B.B. King, Steve Allen
**D:** Joe Dante, John Landis, Carl Gottlieb, Peter Horton, Robert Weiss
**P:** Robert K. Weiss
**C:** Daniel Pearl
**S:** Michael Barrie
**M:** Marshall Harvey

Yet another plotless, loosely constructed media spoof. This one depicts the programming of a slipshod television station as it crams weird commercials and shorts around a comical '50s sci-fi flick. The title piece is a clever mix of '50s cheapie sci–fi-complete with a moon expedition. The music adds to the scene as it parodies the period too. Other highlights include the skits "Son of the Invisible Man," "Video Pirates," and the Dante-directed "Damaged Lives/Sex Madness." There's even a funny Siskel/Ebert parody and Henry Silva doing a side-splitting takeoff of Leonard Nimoy and *In Search Of . . .* This low-budget piece of insanity lingered on the shelf for nearly a year before receiving a theatrical release, and is now finally finding new life on video.

---

### Director Joe Dante in the Hot Seat

| | |
|---|---|
| The Burbs (1989) | Innerspace (1987) |
| Gremlins(1984) | Twilight Zone: The Movie (1983) |
| Gremlins 2: The New Batch (1990) | |

*Life in outer space isn't so bad, after all.*

**R**esist the temptation or you may end up like Pete and Mary and Ken.

*Doctor (Paul Bartel) in the ominous
last line of the movie*

# Beverly Hillbillies

**(1993) 93m PG**

Jim Varney, Erika Eleniak, Diedrich Bader, Cloris Leachman,
Dabney Coleman, Lily Tomlin, Lea Thompson, Rob Schneider
**D:** Penelope Spheeris
**P:** Ian Bryce, Penelope Spheeris
**C:** Robert Brinkmann
**S:** Jim Fisher, Lawrence Konner, Mark Rosenthal, Jim Staahl
**M:** Lalo Schifrin

Hear the sounds of the twanging banjo, see the old jalopy putz-
ing down a tree–lined avenue in posh Beverly Hills toting a very
out–of–place, motley crew. Yes, Jed and all his kin are back and
this time they're in the fee–tures. If you're looking for a heapin'
helpin' of roadkill stew and a down–home hoedown, this is the
movie to serve it up 'cause it's even dumber than the classic TV
sitcom. Varney doubles as the good–hearted Jed and Leachman
as the forever crusty Granny. The clan enters town puttering
down the freeway, mistaking another driver's middle finger
salute as an authentic "Beverly Hills howdy." They then proceed
to happily bid hello in the native way to all the other passing
cars. This is just the beginning of the fish–out–of–water syndrome that the Clampetts encounter. Jethro (Bader) is trying to
find a suitable bride for his lonely but obviously eligible (he's a
billionaire!) bachelor uncle. In walks underhanded gold digger
Thompson, posing as a French governess who seems to be the
perfect role model for daughter Elly May (Eleniak). But watch
out Clampetts—this pretty little thing and her sleazy banker
boyfriend (Schneider) are closing in for the kill. The cast is
rounded out cleverly with Coleman as the uppity Mr. Drysdale
and Tomlin as his prim and proper assistant, Miss Hathaway, who
still has that unexplainable crush on Jethro. Surprise cameos by
Zsa Zsa Gabor (Miss Beverly Hills herself), Dolly Parton, and
Buddy Ebsen (the original Jed) reprising another familiar TV
icon of his, Barnaby Jones, add to the lowbrow fun.

*Howdy, ya'll!*

# Cabin Boy

**(1994) 80m PG-13**

Chris Elliott, Ann Magnuson, Ritch Brinkley, James Gammon,
Brian Doyle-Murray, Russ Tamblyn, Brion James, Ricki Lake,
Bob Elliott, Earl Hofert (David Letterman)

**D:** Adam Resnick
**P:** Tim Burton
**C:** Steve Yaconelli
**S:** Adam Resnick
**M:** Steven Bartek

Welcome to the longest 80 minutes in recent cinema history, a silly fest that occasionally works but gets points for simply existing (what were they thinking?). Taking the helm at last place in this boatload of idiot's delights is not the worst movie of all time, but it's certainly up there with the most inane, unredeemable Hollywood efforts ever, which makes it the perfect choice to close the list. Fancy lad Elliott accidentally boards the wrong boat and finds himself as the new cabin boy for a crew of rude, smelly, obnoxious sailors. What follows is a surreal blend of fish-out-of-water comedy and fantasy that for the most part doesn't work, probably due to the lack of a script. Humor is mostly derived from intentionally cheesy sets coupled with a plot that's obviously not meant to be taken seriously. Highlights include Elliott's show-biz friends that show up briefly; look for Letterman as an old salt trying to sell his monkey, Lake as part of the ship, and real life dad Bob Elliot (of Bob and Ray fame) as the fancy lad's father. Surprisingly produced by Tim Burton, who must have had a vision of the boat in a bathtub and was able somehow to transfer that image to screen intact. At least Letterman got some laughs out of his role during the Academy Awards show—he played a video with an array of big–wig actor buddies trying out his line to hock a stuffed monkey.

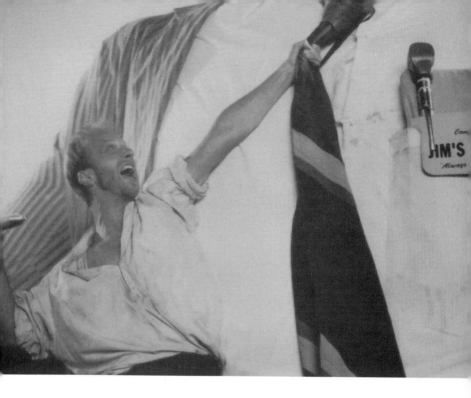

*Elliott bravely attacks giant ogre's tie.*

## Ya wanna buy a monkey?

*David Letterman*

# Classic Idiot's Delight

## Modern Times

**(1936) 87m**
Charlie Chaplin, Paulette Goddard, Henry Berman, Stanley Sanford, Gloria DeHaven, Chester Conklin **D:** Charlie Chaplin

One of the last of the great silents. Funny-but-sad commentary on the man vs. machine theme is studied in many university history classes. So why is it on the *Idiot's* list? Well, as anyone knows, recent movies tend to be pretty dumb, but they are often influenced by earlier works. So no list of silly and dumb movies can leave out Chaplin, one of the original greats. He's a factory employee who works the assembly line tightening an endless amount of nuts to steel plates. Sneezing, he misses a bolt, and the line speeds up to a frantic pace, like the famous *I Love Lucy* chocolate factory sequence. Frantic, he chases a secretary out the door because of the nut-like buttons on her blouse and starts to tighten fire-hydrant bolts with his wrench. Mistakenly taken to jail, he meets Goddard and they fall into suburban fantasies together. Three years in the making, this one is a can't miss for fans of mindless laughter. Enjoy this one simply for the sheer humor, but don't miss the brilliance of Chaplin's social commentary.

*The loveable little tramp*

## Inspector General

**(1949) 103m**
Danny Kaye, Walter Slezak, Barbara Bates, Elsa Lanchester, Gene Lockhart, Walter Catlett, Alan Hale **D:** Henry Koster

*The Inspector General* turns the Gogol play on which it was loosely based into a musical tour-de-force from Kaye. Corrupt officials in a small Russian town are expecting a visit from an Inspector General of the Czar. The politicians immediately mistake an illiterate medicine show helper for the official and they descend on him in force. High comedy follows when each of the men tries to bribe him and Kaye attempts to keep the numerous pols hidden from each other, while stealing all their money. Hilarious song and dance routines by the multi-talented Kaye make this a must-see. Songs include "The Gypsy Drinking Song;" "Onward Onward;" "The Medicine Show;" "The Inspector General;" "Lonely Heart;" "Soliloquy For Three Heads;" "Happy Times;" and "Brodny." Also released as *Happy Times*.

## Sons of the Desert

**(1933) 73m**
Stan Laurel, Oliver Hardy, Mae Busch, Charley Chase, Dorothy Christy, Lucien Littlefield **D:** William A. Seiter

Another fine mess is served as classic comedy duo Laurel and Hardy star as themselves in their best-written film (based on one of their silent two-reelers *We Faw Down*). They're up to no good, trying to find a way to attend the Sons of the Desert convention, even though their wives have forbidden them to go. Faking symptoms of a cold, Ollie and friend pull the "we need a Hawaiian cruise to recover" bit, the wives bite, and the boys are off to their lodge convention in Chicago. But the ship sinks,

## Classic Idiot's Delight

*Smiling pretty for the camera*

*The inimitable W.C. Fields*

they show up on a newsreel film of the convention, and, when the ruse begins to unravel, much mayhem ensues. Noted songs are "Honolulu Baby" and "Sons of the Desert." The L & H fan club took this film's title as their official name. If this one sounds familiar, maybe you remember it being called *Sons of the Legion*, *Convention City*, or *Fraternally Yours*.

### Never Give a Sucker an Even Break

**(1941) 71m**
W.C. Fields, Gloria Jean, Franklin Pangborn, Leon Errol, Margaret Dumont
**D:** Eddie Cline

*The Player* of its day, Fields lampoons Hollywood movie-making as he tries to pitch a story to a movie producer. Partly due to his own frustration with the business of show that was in the process of phasing him out, Fields takes this wild, sometimes surreal parody as far as it will go. Highlights of this almost plotless comedy include a scene where the booze-crazy comedian ejects himself from a plane in mid-flight to retrieve his beloved bottle. Dumont is fabulous as the hot-blooded mother of Fields' love interest, Ouliotta Delight Hemogloben. Something of a cult favorite, it's Fields at his most unleashed. Ends with a classic car chase.

### Francis the Talking Mule

**(1949) 91m**
Donald O'Connor, Patricia Medina, ZaSu Pitts, Ray Collins, John McIntire, Eduard Franz, Howland Chamberlain, Frank Faylen, Tony Curtis **D:** Arthur Lubin

This movie has barn-yard comedy corralled as the first in a series of farmy funnies. This asinine adventure takes us to Burma where dense G.I. O'Connor hooks up with a talking mule called Francis. The joke is that Francis is smarter than any of the humans. Francis, of course, decides only to speak to O'Connor, not unlike the dancing frog of *Bugs Bunny* fame. The pair wreak havoc on the enemy and O'Connor dutifully reports

*Bud and Lou.*

every incident to his C.O., who repeatedly sends him to the rubber room. Eventually, the ass submits, and speaks to the general when commanded, letting O'Connor off the hook. These comedies were box office boffo and were the inspiration for director Lubin's later television series, *Mr. Ed.*

## Africa Screams

**(1941) 84m**
Bud Abbott, Lou Costello, Shemp Howard, Hillary Brook, Max Baer, Buddy Baer, Joe Besser, Frank Buck, Clyde Beatty
**D:** Charles D. Barton

Grandfathers of farce, Abbott and Costello, clown their way through in this unheralded, independent film. The Tsars of zaniness have outwitted themselves again as bookstore clerks trying to impress a pretty customer interested in an old book on Africa. Bud successfully convinces the evil Diana (Brooke) that Lou is a big game hunter and expert jungle navigator. After they fake their way through African Map Making 101, she is convinced, and Diana and her henchmen (the Baer brothers) abduct the duo and take them to the jungles of Africa, forcing them to lead her to a specific tribe where her gang has hidden a cache of diamonds. Of course, no classic comedy would be complete without employing lots of otherwise unemployed actors in gorilla suits, and certainly not one set in Africa! Good production value and a supporting cast of familiar comedy faces.

# Title Index

# Cast Index

# Writer Index

**Rick Copp**
The Brady Bunch Movie, *120*

**Wayne Crawford**
Valley Girl, *83*

**Cameron Crowe**
Fast Times at Ridgemont High, *42*

**Rusty Cundieff**
Fear of a Black Hat, *118*

**Michael Curtis**
...And God Spoke, *136*

**Rodney Dangerfield**
Back to School, *70*

**Joe Dante**
Rock 'n' Roll High School, *101*

**David Dashev**
Summer School, *142*

**John De Bello**
Some Like It Hot, *56*

**Rudy DeLuca**
Caveman, *172*

**Costa Dillon**
Some Like It Hot, *56*

**Nancy Dowd**
Slap Shot, *74*

**Robert Downey Sr.**
Putney Swope, *114*

**Brian Doyle–Murray**
Caddyshack, *6*

**Hal Dresner**
Zorro the Gay Blade, *168*

**Russ Dvonch**
Rock 'n' Roll High School, *101*

**Blake Edwards**
The Party, *108*
The Pink Panther, *24*

**Laurice Elehwany**
The Brady Bunch Movie, *120*

**Michael Elias**
The Jerk, *10*

**Bobby Farrelly**
Dumb & Dumber, *14*

**Peter Farrelly**
Dumb & Dumber, *14*

**Jim Fisher**
The Beverly Hillbillies, *180*

**Bill Fishman**
Tapeheads, *106*

**Jeff Franklin**
Summer School, *142*

**Bob Gale**
1941, *104*
Used Cars, *72*

**Allen (Gooritz) Garfield**
Bananas, *84*

**David Giler**
The Money Pit, *130*

**Terry Gilliam**
Monty Python and the Holy Grail, *20*
Monty Python's Life of Brian, *66*

**Dan Goldberg**
Meatballs, *148*
Stripes, *62*

**Bob Goldthwait**
Shakes the Clown, *119*

**Carl Gottlieb**
Caveman, *172*
The Jerk, *10*

**Christopher Guest**
This Is Spinal Tap, *8*

**Charlie Haas**
Gremlins 2: The New Batch, *64*

**Jeff Harris**
Johnny Dangerously, *124*

**Phil Hartman**
Pee Wee's Big Adventure, *26*

# THE 100 DUMBEST MOVIES OF ALL TIME
## Writer Index

# Director Index

# Category Index

# Category Index